THE NATURE OF WOMAN

When the Feminine Is Ready,

the Masculine Responds

Peggy Funk Voth

Published by Daughter of Esther Books, March, 2021
ISBN: 9781777598006

Editor: Danielle Anderson
Proofreader: John De Freitas
Portrait Photographer: Ezra Voth
Typeset: Greg Salisbury
Book Cover Design: Tara Eymundson

About the Cover
The image on the front cover portrays a dynamic of the female psyche. A woman's inner masculine lives in the shadow-world of her unconscious. When her ego is developed enough to engage this energy, her inner man gets behind her, supporting her values and her endeavours. Such union brings a radiance to the woman's presence, allowing her to shine.

Dedicated to the late Daryl Sharp
(1936–2019)
who was my first training analyst,
and whose words of pithy wisdom
led to this book
and became the subtitle:
"When the feminine is ready, the masculine responds."

Table of Contents

Preface

I am Peggy, daughter of Esther, granddaughter of Sarah. All three of us are products of a patriarchal religion which taught that women must remain silent because female intelligence is inferior to male intelligence. Because women's ways are unreliable and might lead others astray. Because female concerns are fluff—insignificant and not to be taken seriously. We were "good" women in that we were compliant, submissive, and hardworking. We bore and raised children, let our husbands take the lead, and did not air our sufferings.

With each generation, we became more and more disembodied, cut off from the depths of our feminine natures. A stain of unworthiness bled into every daughter at birth through the curse of silence.

When I was six years old, an accident required numerous stitches on my most private parts. My feet were tied to the stirrups of the examination table, my hips and shoulders held still by nurses. My mother left the room before the drunk doctor stitched me up without anything to dull the pain. I remember calling for my mother as the lights above me swam in wavery circles, yet she didn't come.

Thirty years later, my mother, Esther, told me that when the doctor peeled back the layers of my injury and she saw the damage done to me, she passed out. She also shared another story. When she was in elementary school, she rode to school with her older brother, who was in high school. On the way, Allen sometimes stopped by a bridge, took her down to the river below, and used her sexually. Esther begged her own mother to let her ride the school bus rather than go along with Allen, to no avail. My grandmother, Sarah, was married to a man held in high esteem by the religious community in which they lived. Her husband and her church expected her to be silent and obedient. When she displeased my grandfather, he trampled her flower beds, which were her pride and joy. Allen was my grandfather's favourite child.

Even if Sarah had a hunch about what was happening to her daughter, it may have seemed normal to her; lots of boys did things to their sisters. Furthermore, she had no language for what was being done to my mother. The term "sexual abuse" came into existence during my adulthood, decades after my grandmother was gone.

My mother went unconscious when I needed an alert adult to protect me from further trauma because she could not bear what she saw. It may have triggered her own childhood feelings of helplessness, created by those times when her brother took her under the bridge. The nurses also went along with the doctor's sketchy decision to withhold anesthetic; after all, he had power over their livelihood.

When I came home after the stitching, my family didn't know how to relate to me. Everyone seemed to be embarrassed. We didn't even have words for the parts of me that had been hurt—so personal, so hidden. At dinnertime, I sat on a chair topped with a donut-shaped cushion in the corner of the living room while everyone else ate in the kitchen.

Time passed. I healed, yet that trauma, in its many layers, set my path. I knew something was missing in my surroundings and in my life. I longed for . . . what?

I did not know, but my yearning was intense. Constant. Deep.

Introduction

For as long as I can remember, I ached for something I could not name. In midlife, I spent a year going into solitude for three full days every month. There I stumbled upon what I was looking for, but I still had no name for it. Feeling overwhelmed by what I had encountered during my retreats, I began seeing a Jungian analyst. Therapy led me into studying Carl Jung's psychology, which gave me language for what I had sought and found: the feminine.

A major element in Jungian psychology is the acknowledgement that the feminine aspect of the human psyche exists, has been neglected, and must be brought into awareness. Having worked as a therapist with thousands of people—both men and women—over the past twenty-five years, I agree with Jung's emphasis on valuing the inner feminine and developing a relationship with it. That line of approach is part of what drew me into becoming a Jungian analyst.

My training involved eight semesters of coursework, a psychiatric practicum, supervised clinical work, and comprehensive exams. At the centre of the training was hundreds of hours of personal analysis. Through this combination of formal education and deep inner work, I gained, to some degree, an understanding of the feminine nature.

The feminine is a way of knowing and relating that inhabits every being: women, men, animals, insects, plants, and stars. It is the wellspring of existence, bringing life into the world and then nurturing and preserving it. Intimately involved with survival, the feminine energy gets into the midst of situations, experiencing them through feeling and joining with them. On a mundane level, the feminine principle is what enlivens a workplace, turns a house into a home, and bonds a family or community. The feminine energy stirs us through beauty, visual appeal, imagination, and emotional arousal.

While the feminine births and nourishes life, the masculine serves life through focus, initiative, and action. The masculine makes the house that the feminine transforms into a place of warmth and connection. Impersonal and detached, the masculine provides opportunity for growth, often seen in fathers who allow their children to do things that seem too risky to the mother. The masculine establishes security by marking and defending boundaries. Like sperm fertilizing the egg, masculine energy sets things in motion, creating the structure within which living can happen.

The inner masculine and feminine are laws of Nature — predetermined principles, unerring and inevitable, that are built into our lives. Each behaves according to its essence, and each is programmed into our psyches. We can discover these principles, explore them, and learn about them, but we cannot escape them, for they are within us. The feminine flows closer to the surface in women whereas the masculine moves more freely in men.

Society attempts to rid us of any aspects of these principles that are seen as undesirable, especially in women, but it rarely succeeds. For instance, our social systems of family, education, and religion try to train aggression—part of the masculine imprint of protecting life—out of us with limited success. They also shame woman-talk and dismiss views that don't make logical sense. Yet these feminine orientations still continue, if only internally.

Many of us women are better versed in the ways and wiles of an artificial or socialized feminine than our natural way of being. Magazines, movies, and other women tell us how to be sexy, how to catch a man, how to keep a man, how to reach orgasm, and how to dress for power. We are surrounded by beauty tips, health tips, fashion tips, homemaking tips, and mothering tips. These may be useful at times, but they are superficial and get us only so far. There is more to the feminine than this limited view provides. I call the feminine core that remains untouched by society the "natural" feminine.

Despite this cultural rejection of the feminine nature, women's inborn instinct toward the furtherance of life shines through. We make a baby out of sperm, create a meal out of groceries, turn a house into a home. We pour our heart into transforming a wedding into a marriage. It is our nature to enlarge what is given to us.

This natural feminine was within me and around me all along, but for many years I was disconnected from her. Consciously, I knew nothing about her. My culture stripped her of value, of importance. My religion despised her. Throughout generations, my family dismissed her, even abused her in various ways—yet by virtue of being a rural people, they kept a link to her. As farmers, they depended on and partnered with Mother Earth, the source of life and the feminine bestower of survival.

My childhood injury traumatized both my body and my psyche. Being a girl seemed dangerous. Unsafe. I could be hurt; I had been hurt. As a young adult, I began avoiding gatherings of women, instead seeking the company of men. Feeling embarrassed by the ways of ladies—what they talked about, the roles they filled—I faked an interest in male-oriented activities like dismantling, comparing, labelling, statistics, and competition. These choices went against a grain deep within me. What truly engaged my curiosity were the parts of life involving womanhood, but it took a long time for me to admit this to myself.

Over time, as I gained language for and understanding of the feminine nature, my own female wound became a symbol of the suffering inflicted on the archetypal feminine and those in whom she dwells most fully: girls and women. My journey along this line of discovery has developed into a passion for the presence of the feminine. My rejection of her is being redeemed, corrected. I admire the beauty, strength, and wisdom in women. I write for women, work with women, enjoy their inclination toward relatedness and inclusion. I desire to help myself and other women embrace our feminine natures in every way.

A number of people have cautioned me against publishing this book. They have warned, "No one wants to read about someone else's experiences," "Feminists will not agree with you," and "It would not be good for your clients to know these things about you." None of this advice came out of a conscious desire to silence the feminine, but that was, in effect, the message. The conscious belief of these advisers was that they were protecting me from failure, conflict, or professional mishap. Nevertheless, their words were invitations to remain mute, and by doing so, I would contribute to the censoring that the natural feminine has endured for centuries.

I have listened to the urgings of this book for many years and have decided to break the silence. Here I give voice to the instinctive, inborn, deep feminine through my experiences and understandings of her.

Nevertheless, the creation of this book has had its unique challenges. For instance, I am accustomed to writing papers and theses for school: start with a thesis statement, craft an outline, build a linear case for the topic, use an academic voice. I forced that process onto the first draft, and it was a disaster—scientific, cold, dry, and boring. There was no life in it. The feminine is cyclical and playful; she would not, could not, allow herself to be corralled into the masculine organization of an academic paper. Chapters refused to be written in order; even sections of chapters came to me hodgepodge. Each seemed to demand its own look, own length, own depth, and own place. My rational brain didn't always agree with this approach, but eventually it submitted to the promptings of the feminine.

I also faced some difficulty around word choice. Our language in North America is very masculine in that it is full of action words: fight, drive, achieve, focus, accomplish, lead, build, work. Just do it. Go for it. Give 'er. Push through. Words associated with the feminine tend to be adjectives describing states of Being: receptive, beautiful, fertile, gentle, pregnant, lush, open, gracious. The feminine realm is that of the inner world, and our language communicates this reality. Having more words for masculine activities than for feminine states added a challenge to honouring the feminine content of the book with words appropriate to it.

Furthermore, the material of this book wanted to be juicy and frisky; my inner masculine, who has definite ideas about how things should be, disapproved. One day, at my wits' end and tired of wrestling with my writing, I gave up and ran errands instead. Thank goddess I did!

As I shopped in one store, a child's playmat decorated with a farm scene caught my eye. I bought it, took it home, and mounted it on the wall above my laptop. Thereafter, I stuck the image of a cow or a bull on that mat—depending on which one I was writing about—for every thousand words I wrote. I had the cows in a pasture with a barn and the bulls inside a fenced pasture. Whenever I sent a chapter to my editor, I tacked a cow or a bull onto a lane leading out of the farmyard.

Seeing those pastures fill with cows and bulls motivated me to keep writing, keep releasing cattle into the lane. The mat helped me play at writing. The animal pictures reminded me to stay close to the *nature* of the feminine and masculine forces in the human psyche, the way they existed before they became domesticated into social conformity. To that end, the behaviours of the cow and the bull appear throughout the book.

To help explain the concepts I am presenting, I have included some of my own personal experiences as well as those of other women in my life. A pivotal experience in bringing me back to my own self as a female was the year of monthly solitary retreats that I took in my fifties. At the time, my children were launching, my career was blossoming, and my marriage was stable, but I felt dead inside. When I came across a book called *The 13 Original Clan Mothers* by Jamie Sams, I found a remedy for my angst. Sams states that when a woman embraces regular times of withdrawal, in which she has nothing to attend to except her own natural rhythms, she returns to her visionary nature and spiritual sensitivity. My solitudes did that for me. This book includes some of the gleanings from those retreats, and drawings done during my solitary times are interspersed between the chapters.

Many women I know speak of a desire to understand what the feminine is, to live out of the feminine, to embody her more fully. Sometimes we manage, in a flash, to respond from our connection to her. Stories of these moments from the lives of clients, friends, and myself are also sprinkled throughout the pages of this book.

Modern life is one-sided in its orientation toward the masculine principle, which has thrown us out of balance. We see this in poverty, bloodshed, the disappearance of species, and the contamination of our soil, air, and water. Life on our planet needs the harmonizing effect of the masculine's counterpart, the feminine, with her priority on life. It is through the inclusion of the feminine that our society, culture, and world will find the satisfaction that comes with equilibrium.

The same is true for us as individuals. Whether man or woman, attaining the fullness of who we are requires that we embrace the feminine nature within ourselves. This involves claiming our feelings and the needs of our bodies. It requires openness to the cyclical nature of life, to not knowing, and to the upsurge of creative instinct in the moment it arises. It means taking the advancement of life into account when making decisions.

Fulfilling our purpose, feeling complete within ourselves, living a meaningful life—all these things that bring a sense of wholeness—come through connecting with the natural feminine. This is because the feminine principle serves the furtherance of life.

Feminine potency exists in every life-form regardless of the sex, but it flows most easily in girls and women. It is therefore females who will take us into a new ordering of priorities, into leading the masses with care, into boardrooms of dialogue, cooperation, inclusion, and peace. There are paths to be blazed, wisdom to be spoken, native knowledge to be valued, mending and tending to be done. The world as it is currently composed—its societies devoid of the feminine for so long—cannot right itself alone. Only the inclusion of the feminine can bring the current masculine dominance to its senses.

Unfortunately, growing up in a patriarchal society does a number on us. We are encouraged to do, do, do at the expense of Being, which is a feminine quality. For a long time, women have only had men as role models for how to function in the outer world. Molding ourselves after men has resulted in many of us becoming mini-men, or inferior men. Yet the world does not need imitation men; it needs full-hearted, full-throated, full-blooded women!

This book attempts to show what it looks like to be rooted in our feminine origins. The natural feminine expresses itself through our bodies, our cycles, our instincts, and our knowings. As we connect with the inner feminine, we come home to ourselves. Life does not become easier, but we live it with more ease. My hope is that the information and stories offered here help you, the reader, to contact the feminine source of life that lies deep within you.

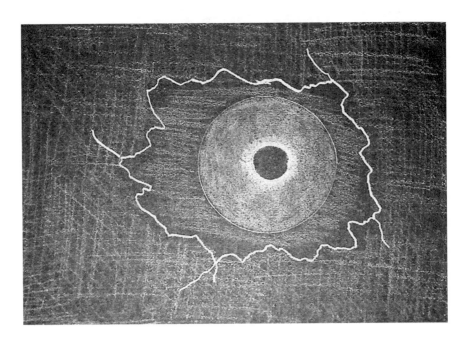

Being Observed

"The receptive nature of the feminine attracts, arouses, and
invites engagement."
–Peggy Funk Voth

1

The Cow

Females of every age need to feel safe enough to speak and move freely through our days: free of male evaluation, free of inner judgment, free of verbal and physical violence. Centuries of negative labels slapped onto feminine ways of seeing, being, and thinking have eroded our confidence in our natural feminine selves. Many of us don't even know the general characteristics that belong to the feminine nature.

My use of the words "natural" and "nature" refers to what exists within us from birth. There are inborn physical traits like genitals, bone structure, fat distribution, muscular abilities, and hormones specific to the sex of the body. There are also psychological characteristics that accompany the infant: what the child notices or is drawn to, the switching of emotions on and off, the use of the body, and the style of responsiveness to people, animals, and danger are a few examples.

These natural traits don't just exist in humans; they are found in the animal world as well. Growing up on a quarter section of fields and pastures with a father who worked in a factory but loved the land, I developed a sacred connection to Nature. The sounds and smells and habits of cats, dogs, chickens, pigs, and cattle were familiar to me. Through this experience, I have seen that all animals and humans share the same natural instincts, but the way in which women and men express those instincts differ. Danger triggers the instinct to survive in both animals and humans, yet male animals fight or flee while female animals show more complex behaviours that are dependent on the situation. They may hide (if they are pregnant and can't flee), distract (in order to protect a young one), or group together (finding safety in numbers).

Humans are different from animals in that we are conscious of ourselves; animals act out of pure instinct while humans have developed some ability to manage our responses. Nevertheless, the patterns that are exhibited by animals give us clues as to what is "natural" behaviour, which then provides us with information about the unsocialized "nature" of the feminine or masculine way of being.

One animal we can consider in this way is the cow. In her unself-conscious way of Being, the cow reminds us of two basic qualities of the feminine that flow in us as women: a sense of timing and an ability to receive. The cow rules the pasture through these parts of her nature. I am well aware that women are sometimes referred to as "cows" in a derogatory way; we do not need to accept such dismissal of us, nor the diminishment of an animal that has nourished humanity for ages. My intention in writing this book is to correct the slandering of the natural feminine, which inhabits all life.

The feminine feature of timing can be seen in the cow's fertility pattern. A cow cycles in and out of fertility approximately every twenty-one days until she conceives, and the actual period during which she can conceive in each cycle lasts anywhere from two to twenty-four hours. These hours of peak fertility are known as being in "heat." The cow becomes restless during this time, bawling, pacing, or mounting other cows. She may instinctually abandon her calf and join other cows who are in heat in order to attract a bull; after all, there is "power" in numbers! Or she may roam about in a state of disorientation. She wants something. Whether she knows what that is or not, her body is ready to couple.

The other aspect of the feminine—receptivity—is demonstrated by the cow's behaviour. Only when her cycle reaches its hottest does the cow stand still and open to the penetrating activity of the bull-masculine. Her inner egg lies ready to receive fertilization. The pantry of her uterus is stocked, her cervix unlocked, her vaginal tunnel soft and contracting upward to admit the penis and usher the sperm in. The cow's stillness puts out a welcome mat.

With cows, everything is instinctual and physical. Simple. Straightforward. For humans, readiness is more complex. Emotions and beliefs become attached to past experiences while socialization informs our readiness. Sometimes, a woman's body refuses to cooperate in a literal way.

Neither my husband nor I had sex before marriage. On our wedding night, he was curious and primed to go. I was also curious and thought I was primed to go. Not so much. For three nights and days, intercourse was impossible—no matter what we did, he could not enter. A long time later, I found out that there is a term for what was happening: vaginismus. This is when the muscles of the vagina contract so tightly that nothing can get in.

My sexual instinct was activated, but so was my protection instinct, set off by the trauma to that part of my body at age six. I was not consciously afraid; I was not thinking about being stitched up without anaesthetic. However, the instinct to keep my body safe was on full alert.

There were psychological reasons at play as well. For one, we unwisely watched the movie "One Million Years BC" starring Raquel Welsh during our honeymoon. Her voluptuous body, almost fully exposed, would make any man beside himself with arousal. I, on the other hand, left the theatre feeling flawed from head to toe.

Another psychological effect came from the numerous ways in which I had betrayed myself throughout our relationship. Filled with feelings of inferiority and self-judgement, I kept my fears and hopes to myself as I joined Steve in whatever he enjoyed, from drinking Coke to playing Rummy to singing in the church choir—all of which I hated. I did not question his choices, did not challenge his opinions, even when they seemed wrong to me. Believing that he knew best simply because he was a man left me embarrassed about my inner responses to whatever was happening. My likes and dislikes, my desires, my feelings about what he said or did or didn't do all seemed unwarranted, and so I stayed silent. In other words, I did not let Steve in, emotionally or otherwise.

After three days and nights, those vaginal muscles relaxed and allowed entrance. I'm not sure what changed, but suddenly we were having sex. My vagina has not locked down since, not even during medical examinations.

Sexual pain occurred three other times in my life: after two births, and after a vaginal hysterectomy. All of these required stitches. For these it was pain that I experienced, not refusal of entrance. The stitches were always given a full six weeks to heal, but intercourse was quite painful for a significant length of time afterward. A few years after I had endured all of that, a doctor mentioned the "husband stitch" to me.

Husband stitch? What is that?

It is a disgrace. It is abuse. Without telling me, without asking me, an extra stitch or two was put in place after the births and hysterectomy to tighten my vaginal opening for my *husband's pleasure*. The doctor told me it was common practice. Goddess damn that practice! It should be a woman's choice, if it's done at all. At the very least, a woman should be told that it has been done so that she knows the source of her new pain.

I still feel outraged…

The opportunity for receptivity is easy to miss. While it is associated with women, due in part to the structure of our sexual parts, for many of us receptivity requires conscious development. We have grown up in a culture that devalues it, with mothers whose natural receptivity has been quashed by the emphasis on doing, being on time, looking good, and raising productive children. Added to that are the expectations that we pull our weight financially, assert ourselves, and compete in the career world or against each other as attractive, independent women. How easy it is to become so busy that we don't take the time to be present and responsive. How easy it is to drown our receptive natures in practicalities—to repeat the brusque refusal of opportunities out of "common sense," as we saw our mothers and aunts do.

On a psychological level, there is a subtle quality to an attitude of receptivity. It happens in the moment, infusing our experience with meaning and often with emotional intimacy.

Only toward the last years of my mother's life did I begin to notice the little ways in which she denied my father the privilege of giving to her. One day, I was with her in a store when she saw a doll in a candy-striper outfit. It was on sale for five dollars. She touched the doll, picked it up, then put it back. On the way out of the store, she handled it again, commenting on how beautiful it was. When we got home, I told my father about the doll and my mother's attraction to it; he went out and bought it. When he gave it to her, she said, "Oh, you shouldn't have. I like it, but it's not important."

My mother's unreceptive attitude cost my father, and her, much more than money. My father was denied the pleasure of pleasing my mother; she missed out on feeling cared for, seen, and valued. This was a miscarriage of a possible intimacy.

I myself have fallen into this trap of rejecting an act of affection. Shortly after my father died, I was in a grocery store with my husband. He spotted a bouquet of sunflowers and wanted to buy it for me. The timing was right, as was the bouquet: my father loved sunflowers, and I was still raw from his death and full of sadness. Those flowers would have eased my pain and given tribute to the memory of my father, but I looked at the price tag and said, "No, they cost too much."

Sometimes we reject what others offer us because we do not feel worthy. Perhaps, as a child, we were not seen for who we were. Some of us were just part of "the kids" and not acknowledged as an individual. This can put us into a double bind. If we have not been met and received by others, it can be difficult to appreciate ourselves. Yet if we do not accept and value ourselves in all our faults and imperfections, we cannot trust the acceptance and appreciation others express toward us as being real or sincere.

In the example above, I couldn't let my husband in emotionally. His desire to buy the sunflowers for me showed that he was "feeling with" me and wanted to comfort me; he was receiving me in my grief. I turned down his attempt to ease the heaviness of my heart because I did not feel deserving of a little bit of money—did not feel worthy of his compassion.

Saying "no" denied both my husband and me an experience of closeness. His sensitivity would have been received; my sorrow would have been honoured. When I realized what I had done a couple of days later, I felt remorse and wanted to undo it. But the moment was gone, scattered into thin air. All I can do is be aware now, for those kinds of moments are all around me.

Receptivity is necessary for the creation of new life—not just a physical baby, but also the birth that can come from embracing a creative idea, an insight, or a spiritual vision. The feminine is fertile in mysterious ways, and being open to her timing can introduce us to ourselves in surprising ways.

In the cow pasture, receptivity depends on the inner timing of the cow's fertility cycle. During the non-fertile period of her cycle, she is calm, content, and disinterested in coitus. As she approaches fertility, she becomes restless and skittish. When she reaches the peak of her "heat," she behaves in a receptive manner which attracts, arouses, and invites engagement with the bull.

Similarly, midlife often brings feelings of dissatisfaction, frustration, and unease. We feel disoriented, as we should, for the second half of life is not meant to be a repeat of the first. The unlived life—the dreams and yearnings we once had—asks to be remembered and lived.

For women, our creative life can expand once the childbearing years come to a close. As concerns related to fertility and childrearing dry up, previous interests may return and our world outside the home may flourish. Like the cow, we come into a desire for fruitfulness. Restless discontent signals a readiness in our psyches to become juicy with potential. Our part is to tolerate the building tension and trust that when the time is right, what needs to happen will happen.

This receptive waiting lubricates the way to psychological fertilization. When we open to our inner timing, a conception of the moment, a visitation pregnant with meaning, or a sudden birth of feeling can occur. We expand with new life.

My midlife skittishness took me into solitude. Slowing down and clearing a few days every month to be alone with my own rhythms made space for the feminine to show up. One day, about halfway through my year of solitary retreats, she came to me through my body.

Solitude – My Female Body

One morning, my eyes fall on a drawing I made the day before. Every time I've looked at this image, I've felt a slow stirring of energy behind and above my pubic bone. This happens again in this moment—a powerful uncoiling deep within my pelvic region. I note it as I sit down at my table to do some creative writing.

I write for thirty minutes. As I write, I feel occasional stirrings and tuggings—sort of like vibrations—in my uterine area.

I tend the woodstove and then lie down on the couch to do some belly-breathing. Taking deep breaths that fill my belly first, then my diaphragm, and finally my lungs, I visualize my torso as a balloon. Exhaling, I push the air up from my belly first, then the diaphragm area, before finally releasing the air in my lungs. I do this for a long time, maybe fifteen minutes. As I lie there, still and quiet, I notice a feeling of strong sexual energy in my lower abdomen. I relax into the couch and sleep for a moment.

A humming pulsation in my pelvis wakes me. My breasts feel heavy. I get up, stand before the mirror and pull off my clothes. My breasts look full, substantial. My abdomen appears ripe and taut. I feel like I need to pee, but the sensation is behind and below my bladder.

The inner vibrations increase. At the same time, weak nausea disturbs my stomach. As I head for the toilet, I become quite light-headed.

Not knowing whether I'm going to pee, vomit, or pass out, I step into the shower, figuring it can accommodate all three if necessary. I half-squat to get my head between my knees, hoping to reduce the light-headedness.

As I bend forward, I put pressure on my abdomen and a stream of fluid gushes out between my legs—clear as water but a tad denser, carrying the fragile scent of rain. I watch the fluid pour from me with surprise and amazement. I don't know what's happening, am not sure what the fluid is, but I know it's not urine.

The nausea and dizziness pass. I straighten up and weakness rolls over me.

After a quick shower, I towel myself down, feeling very compassionate toward my body. I spread lotion all over myself, touching with feather strokes the veins showing on my legs. I notice my thin skin going crepey in areas and murmur, "It's okay." Caressing the lumps and bumps of age with a touch soft as a whisper, I recognize the faithfulness of my body. Love for it sweeps through me.

Somewhere inside me, the bottom drops out. All my energy leaves, and I'm exhausted. I wrap myself in a terry-cloth robe, crawl into bed, and sleep.

Journal Entry, A Few Hours Later

I want to make peace with my body. I've observed my outer body from afar, either in a mirror or as an objective observer detached from myself. I've watched my body move, fill out my clothes, shape itself into a pleasing, postured pose. I've evaluated its every performance. My body became an entity unto itself that was cut off from the earth, separate from "me," disconnected from its surroundings. It has been alone on a stage of floodlights.

Today is the first time I've seen my body as my own. I've seen its scars and spots and translucence before, but with a judging eye. Today, each scar is part of *me*, each spot is *mine*. I see the skin stretched across my bent knee, and it is *my* skin. The eyes peering back at me from the mirror are *my* eyes. I'm not looking at a body, I'm looking at *me*.

The recognition elates me and frightens *me*.

My body came from my mother—not only out of her body, but also sheltered within her as the unseen influences of her egg and my father's sperm determined me as a female. They gave me a body with physical similarities to my father (bone structure, eye colour, a double-jointed thumb) and biological features that identify me with my mother (hormones, genitals, brain chemistry). My sex was a mystery until I revealed myself at birth.

I am my parents' firstborn, and I was wanted. I know that my mother fantasized about me because she named me after a character in her favourite radio soap opera. This tells me our time together before birth was romantic for her, something that is important for the female psyche.

Without prompting, an expectant woman's inner world generates fantasies. They come while she folds the little pieces of clothing, while lining a dresser drawer, while choosing curtains and wall decals for the baby's room, while cradling her growing belly in her hands or lying awake at night because she can't find a comfortable position. Such daydreaming is important for the mother-baby duo. It prepares the woman's psyche to welcome the newborn, to bond with it, to open her arms and heart. It fortifies her for labour, for the endurance needed during years of active mothering, for the many challenges that will crop up as the child learns to live in the outer world and the mother learns to live with the child.

A centuries-old ritual believed to originate in Africa honours this psychological process of daydreaming on the part of the mother. There is a story that in a village far way, the birth date of a child is not counted from when the child is born, nor even from when it is conceived, but rather from the day that the child is a thought in its mother's mind.

When a woman of this community decides that she will have a baby, she goes off and sits under a tree by herself. She listens until she can hear the song of the spirit-child that wants to be born to her. After she has heard the song of this child, she goes back to the man who will be the father and teaches it to him. When they make love to physically conceive the baby, they sing the song of the child as a way to invite him or her into existence.

When the mother is pregnant, she teaches the child's song to the midwives and the old women of the village. These are the women who attend the birth of the babe, and they sing the child's song during birth to welcome the human creature struggling to be born.

As the little one grows up, the other villagers are taught the child's song. When the youngster falls or hurts its knee, someone picks the lad or lass up and sings their spirit-song to comfort them. When the teenager does something wonderful or goes through the rites of puberty, the people of the village sing the youth's song to honor the adolescent. In response to faulty actions, the song is sung to remind the wrongdoer of the beauty and goodness of his or her personal essence.

This continues throughout the person's life. In marriage, the songs of the bride and the groom are sung together. When the individual is lying in bed, ready to die, all the villagers know his/her song, and they sing it to that person for the last time.

My mother did not sit under a tree and listen for my song, but her desire for children suggests that she daydreamed about being a mother even before she became pregnant. Not only did her family and community expect her to become a mother, but she herself wanted to be one. Her love of children was evident throughout her life. However, she and I were very different in ways that left me feeling unseen and unknown. She wanted children, but did she want *me*? Did she want the me that I turned out to be? This was the central question that bubbled up during one of my solitary retreats.

Solitude – Spirit Song

Journal Entry

What song did my spirit sing when I agreed to come to Earth? Did my mother hear my song as she carried me in her womb? I think that if she'd been listening, she might have heard my spirit say this:

I come trailing beauty.
Whatever my fingers touch,
Wherever my steps fall,
Wherever my eyes linger,
Whatever my breath caresses,
Beauty remains there,
Soft. Light. Present.

I see beauty and it springs into being.
I know beauty and offer it to everyone.
I thrive on beauty and it multiplies around me.

Beauty is my name, my essence.
I bring it.
I create it.
I give it.
I live it.
Beauty abounds because I was born.
I am beauty.
Blessed is beauty.
Blessed am I.

Well, that seems arrogant. Pretentious. Self-flattering and puffed up. But what if it's true? Could it be true? If it's not, it at least gives me something to live up to.

If my Spirit-Song had been heard, remembered, taught to others, and sung to me, the strong messages about the inferiority of females would not have filtered into my life. Feeling valued in all my humanness and femaleness and divinity, I would have believed in myself. That didn't happen, but I now know my Spirit-Song. I can sing it, and I do.

May it inform my days forever.

Within small farms like the one I grew up on, individual cows are often given names. We had a Jersey cow called Jewel and a Holstein named Queenie. When I turned fifteen, my father gave me a calf which I named Delight. Raising my own calf taught me things I now see as applicable to the "raising" of a healthy ego in a woman.

For instance, while inner timing and receptivity are prominent characteristics of the cow, a few things must be in place for that timing to function within her. These pre-requisites are maturity, good health, and strength. The cow must be old enough to start cycling, healthy enough to have a natural cycle, and sturdy enough to take the weight of the bull when he mounts her. Together, these conditions determine the young cow's readiness to enter her fertile phase, which prepares her to join with the bull.

A female calf can go into her first heat by the time she's six months old—before she's weaned off her mother's milk. At this age, the adolescent cow, or heifer, is not physically strong enough to bear up under the mass of the bull. Her hind legs will collapse, or her legs, hips, or back could be injured. Her bones, muscles, and tissue are not yet developed enough that she can carry a fetus to full term; if she does, a heifer impregnated before she's a year old often suffers complications in the birth process. In these cases, it's not uncommon for the heifer and/or her calf to die.

The wise farmer puts a heifer who has reached heat too early into a pasture where the bull cannot get to her. She is given time and protection in which to come into the fullness of being a cow—a creature able to conceive, gestate, and birth new life.

Most of us women in North America were subjected to the weight of patriarchal expectations before we had formed strong psychological legs on which to stand. We had little or no protected space where our individuality could develop in a wholesome way. Thrust into an adult world full of masculine bulk, our feminine selves have not borne up well.

For many of us, our inborn ways of understanding, responding, and being have been injured. We do not remember how to be feminine in a natural way for our socialization has taught us to distrust our instincts and intuition—our way of seeing and knowing. Perhaps we've developed the masculine traits of focus and action, but we don't know how to feel or receive, don't know what feminine timing is. We must relearn what true femininity is and how to embrace it and live from that place.

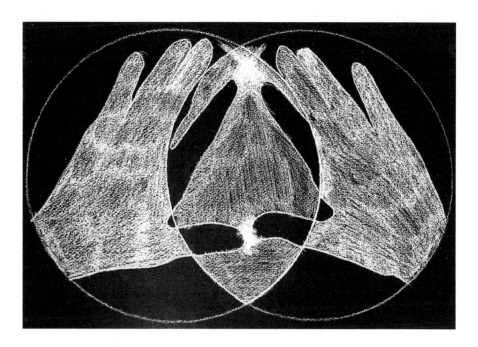

Hands

"When we discover and accept the natural feminine energy within ourselves, we can thrive despite misogyny."
–Peggy Funk Voth

2

Patriarchy and the Handless Maiden

My training to become a Jungian analyst included studying fairy tales because they expose the basic structure of the human psyche. They are collective stories that reflect cultural patterns for they have evolved as societies changed and as storytellers told them. These stories show the native feminine better than explanations or facts do. I have chosen to use a fairy tale called "The Handless Maiden" to illustrate the feminine, the wounding of her by our culture, and some of the paths toward healing.

There once was a miller whose mill had stopped working, plunging him and his family into poverty. One day, an odd man appeared and offered the miller wealth in exchange for what was behind his mill. The miller could easily part with the old apple tree that he knew stood behind it, so he agreed to the deal. The strange man said he would return in three years to collect his payment, then disappeared. When the miller told his wife about their good fortune, she said, "That was the devil, and our daughter was sweeping behind the mill. He didn't want the apple tree, he wanted her."

Three years to the day the pact was made, the maiden bathed, washed her hair, dressed in white, and sat down in the backyard to wait for the devil to collect his due. When he arrived, the girl's cleanliness made it impossible for him to take her. Pointing at the miller, the devil ordered that he not let the maiden bathe, then left.

The maiden obeyed. Her hair became matted; a film of grime covered her skin. She wept daily, her tears streaking her face and washing her hands. Because of this, when the devil returned, he once again could not touch her. Enraged, he ordered the miller to cut off her hands so she could not weep on them. The girl placed her hands, palms up, on the chopping block, and the miller did as he was told. Again, the maiden cried, tears falling on the stumps of her arms. Still having no power over her, the devil left without any threat of coming back.

For the maiden, life as she had known it had come to an end. The miller and his wife wanted to take care of her, to use the wealth they had gained to provide her with a comfortable life, but she refused. Instead, she asked them to bind her arms behind her back and went into the world as a beggar, dependent on the goodness of others. However, instead of taking pity on her, people jeered and threw rocks at her. To stay safe, she slept during the day and travelled by night. Hunger began to stalk her.

One night, the maiden came upon an orchard surrounded by a moat. As she stood, looking and longing, a wraith appeared and carried her across the water and into the orchard. A pear tree bent its branches so that she could eat of its fruit. Unbeknownst to her, this was the king's orchard. When he witnessed this sight, the king fell in love with the maiden. He married her and had silver hands made for the new queen.

The maiden became pregnant; shortly after, the king left for a faraway battle. When the baby was born, the king's mother sent the good news to the king—however, the devil had been watching the maiden. When the messenger fell asleep on the long journey to the king, the devil crept out of the woods and switched the message to convey that the queen had given birth to a creature that was half-dog.

The king was horrified. However, he loved his wife and trusted his mother, so he sent back a message telling his mother to love the queen and take good care of her during this terrible time. Again, the messenger fell asleep on the way. The devil came out from behind a tree and changed the king's message to read, "Kill the queen and her child. Keep the tongue and eyes of the queen to prove that she is dead."

Unable to stand the thought of killing the maiden, the old mother had a deer put to death and its eyes and tongue placed in storage. Then she bound the infant to the maiden's breast, covered her head with a veil and told her to flee for her life. Both women wept as they kissed goodbye.

The maiden wandered for a long while. Eventually she entered a deep, old forest. The wraith that had led her across the moat to the orchard appeared again and took her to a little house, where a very old yet ageless woman opened the door and invited her in. The maiden stayed there for seven years. One day, her child fell into a river near the edge of the woods. Without hesitation, she plunged her silver hands into the water and pulled her child out. Her hands had become human again: flesh and blood warm, able to hold and caress, soothe and flex, touch and feel.

This fairy tale is a stark picture of patriarchy—a form of society that is based on masculine standards and principles to the exclusion of feminine qualities and values. Over a long period of time, this imbalance results in an exchange of human warmth for material wealth.

At the beginning of the story, the father enters into a contract that solves his financial problems but deprives him of his daughter. Psychologically, the daughter represents the feminine principle—the feeling aspect of life. The father assumes the devil wants the tree that stands behind his mill, so to him, the deal seems harmless. But the miller's wife sees through the devil's offer. She sees below the surface. She sees deeply. The devil does not want the tree, he wants the daughter. He wants the vitality that comes with emotional connection: love, compassion, and companionship. However, the wife, the mother of this girl, was not consulted; she had no say in the matter. A deal was struck without her input, and so the feminine was rendered irrelevant and silenced. This initial silencing set the stage for the devil's bargain to play out, taking advantage of the miller's unconsciousness and the girl's innocence.

When the severing of the girl's hands is demanded, she doesn't speak up or resist. She is young and has seen her mother silent and her father compliant. So, she exposes her wrists and positions them for the axe. This is easy to do—even feels normal—when the mother has no voice. By losing her hands, the maiden loses her grasp on her own life.

The handing over of one's life happens in many ways. Sometimes a woman stays in a friendship or partnership in which she cannot be truthful while she changes into someone she doesn't like. Perhaps a woman has one sexual preference but forces herself into another. Maybe she wants to go, do, be something big but stays home and tracks wrinkles on her face. Perhaps she marries for the wrong reasons and cuts off her creative life. Perhaps she doesn't want to marry—maybe she dreams of exploration or solitude or study instead of a wedding and a picket fence—but marries anyway to be "normal" and fit into a society that's made for couples.

There are other nuances to the loss of our hands—our sense of having some authority over our lives. Growing up in a patriarchal society, all of us are socialized into masculine ways of behaving and seeing the world. We learn to be efficient and effective, to push through pain, to ignore our bodies and our feelings. In this fashion, the hands of the feminine side of life are sacrificed. An overbearing emphasis on excellence, output, and material gain cuts off the tender touch and delicate flexibility of the feminine way of handling of things.

When females are not permitted to hold and explore something from all sides, such as ambivalence about marriage or confusion about sexual attractions, we are denied access to a crucial layer of knowing that is unique to the feminine. This knowing is beyond the influence of society. It is beyond reasonable arguments given by the mind. It is inborn, along with our nest of eggs, our hormones, and our uterus. It comes up from the belly through the body, through the heart. It is personal to the woman, attuned to what is good for her at the time. And it is not accepted by our society because it is "irrational." When we ourselves discount our natural knowing, we bare our wrists on the chopping block.

Like most women in North America, my upbringing happened within a patriarchal environment. Religion, schooling, advertisements, and community attitudes taught me to live carefully and to value masculine traits like competitiveness, achievement, and rational thinking. Throughout my childhood, femininity was cloaked in superficial appearances: being thin, speaking quietly, taking up little space. I learned to defer to male opinions for they were accurate and mine were not. Male needs were real and urgent; mine were not.

Growing up in this kind of environment introduces a girl to an artificial femininity. It encourages a woman to abandon her natural way of being and seeing. As girls and as women, the early severing of the feminine feeling for life, the feminine handling of life, separates us from our own intelligence—from our wise instincts.

In many ways, I can identify with the handless maiden. As a child, I was imaginative, intuitive, and open. I enjoyed Nature's seasons and weather and mysteries. But by my late teens, those parts of me felt freakish and I withdrew them from the public eye in order to fit into a world made by and for the masculine way of thinking and doing. I hid my abilities of leadership, thinking outside the box, and intuiting probable outcomes of men's plans, be they my husband's or a politician's. I protected my heart from the affiliation and tenderness I felt toward Nature's rhythms and creatures. In school, I wrote rational papers, made reasonable arguments, and compared myself to others. These are not feminine ways of being. It is women and our sensibilities that bring warmth, spontaneity, and personable interaction to daily life. We humanize the world.

Returning to our story, the girl has been betrayed by her father—by her culture—and she has colluded with it. Now, she is starting to wake up. Something in her knows that if she stays in the shelter of her parents' home—in the shelter of societal approval—the possibility of a life that is truly her own will shrivel and die. She is feeling a desire for love, for creative freedom. She senses a need to take personal responsibility for herself and how she lives.

The maiden launches out on her own to the best of her ability, but the community rejects her. She begins to avoid the public eye. The combination of leaving home and not fitting in thrusts the maiden onto herself. Once she is outside the realm of human activity, she starts figuring out how to survive on her own terms. She travels by foot, connected to the earth, tapping into her own wisdom of hiding during the day and moving at night. Without hands, the maiden lets go of everything—her expectations and plans, her concerns about what others think. She becomes led by instinct, by the psyche within. She depends on life itself to shelter and nurture her, and in learning to trust life in its messy, chaotic state, she is becoming a creature of Nature.

In this state of surrender, help comes from the psyche and from Nature. The soul-spirit arrives unbidden from within and lifts the maiden above her circumstances, then leaves her in Nature's care. A fruit tree responds with nourishment.

Many women tell of some place in Nature that helped them survive a cruel childhood, comforted them through grief, or brought assurance when they felt lost. A grassy spot or a circle of stones. A trail. A riverbank, or the river itself. A branch in a tree. A space beneath a bush. The companionship of a pet. The sun drying her tears. All of these offer themselves like the bough of a pear tree bending to let the maiden eat.

As the miller-father in the story is a figure representing the patriarchy, so the king is a symbol for the ruling values of a society. We all join, in some way, with the views and morals of our surrounding culture. After marrying the king, the maiden is given hands, but they are not her hands. Seemingly crafted out of consideration for her, they nevertheless fall short of her personal power. Silver hands can do some things, but they cannot flex or feel or touch with warmth. They are robotic. Machine-like. They still do not give the maiden the ability to take hold of her life. Without human hands, she remains isolated from authentic communication that rises out of her feelings and experiences.

She cannot relate to others through personal connection.

Having married the king, the maiden is now a queen and has duties to fulfill. Silver hands are more acceptable to the king's people than a woman with no hands at all. So, like many of us, she makes do.

Our silver hands come from the dominant attitudes in our culture. Patriarchy trains women to hide our intelligence, to pursue perfection in how we look or set the table or decorate our house. We learn to take care of others' feelings, to look pretty, and to act mannerly. To stay in the background. To be small. Even touching our own body becomes habitual, detached, done out of necessity rather than out of love and appreciation. Living with an "amputated" understanding of who we are, our actions—though good and nice—have an impersonal feel to them. We cannot yet *do*, or act, out of our own values.

The mechanical nature of my own silver hands showed itself in a lack of spontaneity, a task-focused approach to life, and a deep self-doubt that kept me from doing what I sensed to be right in the moment. For example, mothering my children caused great anxiety because I distrusted my instincts. As a result, I tried to follow the advice of books or imitate my friends in their parenting. I also got severe headaches when leading workshops because I tied myself to the prepared outline and script. I couldn't flow with what unfolded as people interacted with the material and tried to interact with me. In every arena of life, a feeling of being shut down was present within me. I did not feel that I was fully "there."

After the maiden gives birth to her child, the devil shows up again. At the beginning of the story, the devil wanted the young maiden; he wanted the warmth of human connection that the feminine principle brings. When that was denied to him, he demanded the sacrifice of her hands, her ability to take hold of life. Now the devil works to have the maiden killed, and have her eyes and tongue removed. What does he want from her this time?

The feminine principle, though neglected and ignored, always contains the possibility of love and a creative life. As a queen, the young maiden has found a place in the world. She also delivers a newborn child created out of love. Psychologically, this means that her potential is becoming fruitful. Furthermore, that potential is starting to belong to her, not to someone else, not to society. It is hers, and it is slipping beyond the devil's reach. In a last-ditch effort, he demands her tongue and eyes—her feminine gift of seeing the truth, and her feminine courage to speak it.

The devil represents an energy that resists life yet wants the consciousness that enlivens human existence. It is a force that is present both in the outer world and in our inner world. This devilish energy invites us to go to sleep. To stop trying. To give up. To dumb ourselves down, stay small, numb our feelings. There are times when these choices are very tempting, but if we take even a small step away from them, we grow a little deeper into our natural selves.

When I was twenty, I went into a depression that deepened over seven years. During this time, I developed a very strong persona that allowed me to function and look fine to the outside world even though I was desperate and dying inside. I began to lose chunks of time; although I performed my duties, I was absent. I looked with surprise at what I had produced for I could not remember doing it.

This scared me. Terrified me.

My seven-year depression lifted when I talked to a psychiatrist. He was a keynote speaker at a week-long event I attended, and he talked about the impact of childhood experiences on our lives as adults. This was a new concept to me, and each of his talks shook me up. As the retreat was coming to a close, the pain and hopelessness of my depression suddenly felt crushing. The psychiatrist had offered his services to anyone who asked to see him, so I approached him late at night on the last day. Having been around me all week, he was able to name my problem.

"You live in a female body," he said, "yet you have rejected everything feminine. This has put you between a rock and a hard place. Those two realities are closing in on you. You are trapped, and life is being squeezed out of you."

I did not sleep that night. I turned the problem over and over in my mind, knowing and exploring the truth of what he had said. In the morning, I knew I would do something about it, although I wasn't sure what. Now that I saw the misstep I had made, I was able to embrace the pain I suffered. My future was unknown, yet I sensed that what lay before me held more life than death.

The tale of the handless maiden offers clues about how modern women can heal our damaged connection to the feminine nature. It is important to note a thread running through the story. The devil's attempts to possess the maiden's essence for himself have the opposite effect—each suffering adds a new layer to her character.

First, the maiden is set apart from normal life by the devil's instruction to let herself go to the dogs, so to speak. She is not to bathe or clean herself in any way. But she cries; she can't stop crying. This is a good thing, for tears mean that we feel. They are part of the healing process, like the fluid that oozes from a physical wound.

It is not a good sign when a woman cannot cry—something I often see in my therapy room. Women who cannot cry ache inside without any way to ease the pain. They have gone too long without weeping; they had no time for it, no space in which to let it happen. Now their animal-body holds an ocean of sorrow and suffers in polite silence.

Next, the maiden loses her hands—her sense that she can make things happen, that she can shape a life for herself. Thanks to the devil, her parents are wealthy enough to give her a castle and all she needs in it, yet she runs from the possibility. It threatens to define her by her wounding—to keep her wound at the centre of who she is. In refusing the offer to be taken care of, she has a say in her life.

When danger comes for her again, putting her eyes and tongue at risk, she does not want to be deformed further. She once again leaves her familiar life, this time with a bearing that is different. She is disguised, dignified, and unbroken. Her previous ordeals have given her a trust in the timing and the process that accompanies a state of unknowing.

There is wisdom in removing ourselves from our normal lives—from our social calendar, our work responsibilities, our home life, our good-woman identities that suck the lifeblood out of us. These times away get us in touch with our feelings and instincts, providing the physical and emotional space in which our woundedness can heal.

The cycles of stepping outside society's norms and expectations require endurance. It's easy to think that once we have done a difficult piece of work on ourselves, the task is finished. Not so. We may have adjusted to the wound, or found ways to compensate for it, or tended it into a pink layer of new skin only to discover that something else is now threatened. If we are dedicated to coming into a more full and rich femininity, we must endure round after round of private agony and bewilderment. This mirrors the bedevilments that again and again offered the maiden opportunities to listen more closely to guidance from within herself.

A second clue to the healing that can occur is the importance of connection with the natural world. Every awakening that the maiden experiences happens within the context of Nature. She travels by foot, by her own exertion, and at her own pace. She drinks from rivers and streams. She sleeps in the shelter of field furrows, tree groves, and shallow caves. These surroundings take her out of her head and into her emotional gut-knowing. This is what a woman who is separated from her life-giving source needs; Nature abounds with the balm of instinctual living. Furthermore, it was in a natural setting that help comes from the maiden's inner world: a wraith carries her across water to the king's orchard and later leads her to the old woman's house. Both of these happenings introduce a further stage of recovery. Whether child or adult, being close to Nature restores our perspective so that we can see more correctly what is before us.

A further clue about healing is found in the other women in the story. The maiden's mother recognizes the strange man for what he is: a sneak who wants the innocence of her daughter. However, she has no opportunity to intervene. Similarly, the king's mother knows her son, and she knows that something isn't right about the messages coming in his name. Unlike the maiden's mother, though, the king's mother has time to act, and act she does. She binds the babe—the queen's fragile new life—next to the maiden's heart and releases her to Fate. Lastly, an ageless woman opens the door of her little house in the woods, providing a safe and private space in which healing can deepen.

Each of us needs the presence and support of the right women. We need women who accept us but do not coddle us, who name our strengths without being threatened by them. Women who give us airtime without judgment, who can weep with us, who celebrate our victories because they've seen us take lap after lap around the track of our vulnerabilities and injuries. They know how huge a small win is.

We need women who stand by us and with us when we stand by and with ourselves. We need women who speak up in support of an idea that we pitch to a boardroom full of men who then fall silent, clear their throats, and are about to move on to another topic. Sister Comrade, please say, "I think her idea is worth discussing."

At the end of the story, the maiden risks her own safety by plunging her artificial hands into the river to save what she loves. Rescuing her creative potential—her child—is an act of taking hold of her own life. It clinches her healing. Her action reveals a new attitude toward herself and her femininity. She experiences herself as capable, trustworthy, settled within herself, and confident in the worth of her abilities and her choices.

In terms of our lives, saving the child from certain death means opening ourselves to what gives us life. Often this involves breaking away from the script for womanhood that society has provided us. Making this breakaway requires a sturdy ego—one that is rooted deep, connected to the source of feminine life. This was the task of the handless maiden; being products of patriarchy, it is our task as well.

Most women go through a process similar to that of the handless maiden. A wounding occurs, and it follows us into the outer world of adult responsibilities. The ruling principle of our culture accepts us as long as we are attractive and compliant. Then comes a time when that way of being no longer works for us, and we enter the woods through depression or a breakdown or an aching discontent. We may find ourselves withdrawing from the outer world as a result. If we can feel our pain, listen to what it tells us, and trust what we hear, we become more rooted in the deep feminine and our zest for living returns.

We all desire to take our own lives in hand and live out our truest and fullest potential. It is a healthy ego that positions us to move toward and into self-determination. With commitment and an understanding of female ego development, it is possible to return to the femininity that swaddled us at birth.

Tears

"As our ego becomes rooted in the rocky soil of our suffering, we begin to know what to do in the moment."
–Peggy Funk Voth

3

The Female Ego

The ego is the conscious part of our psyche that makes decisions and helps us navigate life. Tasks like choosing where to live or what to wear, making a grocery list, and getting where we need to go are all ones for the ego to perform. A strong ego is curious, humble, and reflective. It means yes when it says yes, means no when it says no. It looks after itself without neglecting others, embraces its longings and shortcomings, likes itself, can be alone, and knows both joy and heartache.

Self-esteem is a primary piece of a person's ego. Basically, there are two parts that make up our self-esteem: self-confidence and self-worth. Both are highly affected by our parents. Our mother and father contribute to the quality of our self-esteem, but each naturally specializes in one aspect.

The first—self-confidence—comes from experiencing ourselves as competent and having our capability recognized. Our culture encourages the development of self-confidence by rewarding achievement, education, and skill. The expertise and affirmations bestowed by the outer world—including parents, teachers, and institutions—make up our reputation with others.

A father influences a girl's ego on the level of activity in the outer world. Teaching his daughter about the outer world helps her feel confident in society. By believing in her mental abilities, affirming her physical activities, and expressing confidence in her as a person, he equips the girl to show initiative, assert herself, and believe in herself.

This kind of relationship with the father, the outer masculine, helps her engage the masculine energy within herself, whose role is to give her a backbone. She is then able to act in her own best interests.

The inner aspect of self-esteem—a sense of worthiness—is hidden but every bit as important as self-confidence. Self-worth is made up of self-trust and self-respect. Keeping our promises to ourselves proves to us that we are trustworthy. Feeling good about how we conduct ourselves builds self-respect. These elements anchor us from within and guide our choices according to personal values. They create our reputation with our self.

A mother's domain is the inner realm; perhaps that is why most children experience their mother as having eyes at the back of her head. Children learn to be comfortable with what rises from within when they see their mother accept their emotions, feelings, and uncanny knowings as well as her own. Through her reactions, we learn to fear or believe our emotions, to dismiss or allow our feelings. The same is true for intuitions, gut-hunches, and body-knowings. All of these offer information about who we are and help us stay safe and sane in the outer world.

A healthy ego enables us to be an authentic presence in the world and to find fulfillment, and so establishing a sturdy ego is a major task of childhood. When such development is incomplete, it then becomes an issue to address in adulthood.

A therapist once diagramed my family history from a psychological viewpoint. In her drawing, she used circles for my grandmothers, aunts, mother, sister, and me. Squares represented my grandfathers, uncles, father, and brothers. She asked me for three words to describe each person—how I experienced them when I was a girl. I began to see some reasons for my lack of self-confidence, my constant self-doubt. On one side of the family, there was no room for ego; all my aunts and uncles were nice, meek, and invisible, striving only for humility. On the other side of the family, the men were puffed up and the women were abused, crushed under the thumb of a male God who spoke only to and through men.

The therapist asked what I thought each of my parents learned about life by growing up in their childhood home. What stories I had been told about my birth and infancy. What the neighbours thought of my family. At the end, she said, "If this whole story were to be made into a movie, what title would you give it?" My response was immediate: Invisible People.

Early in my year of solitary retreats, this family pattern of invisibility caused me some inner conflict. My cabin shared a kitchenette with another. The other cabin was often occupied while I was there, but I rarely encountered those visitors. However, one evening, having barely settled in to begin a retreat, something happened.

Solitude – Men's Voices

What do I hear? Activity in the kitchenette. Men's voices. Then, "Oh wow! Dorothy stocked this place for us! Look—fresh fruit, milk, even hamburger."

It's my food supply they're talking about. I want in the worst way to remain invisible behind my locked door. The last thing I care to do is meet new people, be friendly, act sociable. But men can display a big sense of entitlement. These guys might help themselves to my food.

Should I lay claim to the things I brought? That means standing up for myself. It requires taking the initiative. It involves opening the door and speaking.

Old fears assail me. What's the right way to do this? Should I knock first? What do I say when I open the door? What if my voice fails me?

The flood of uncertainty astounds me. I'm fifty-four years old. I've pastored a church, completed two degrees, facilitated workshops, run a private practice, raised two sons. Yet despite all I've done in my life, this self-doubt feels familiar—old and entrenched. I've worked at allowing myself to be more visible, so I've had much practice at confronting these old fears.

Sometimes I fly through situations like this with ease and grace; this time, I feel struck dumb with panic.

The lure of invisibility beckons with reasonable arguments. "Those men will be gone in the morning—you don't need to show your face." "Lighten up! Your food will be safe. If it's not, make do with what's left." "There you go, being territorial again." "If you introduce yourself, then you also have to extricate yourself. Stay hidden and the evening will be less complicated."

I feel as vulnerable as a child, and I am ashamed of this vulnerability.

After pacing around my cabin a few times, I make a decision and take a few breaths.

I must've yanked the door open, for the poor man jumps. I stick out my hand and try to smile. "I'm Peggy," I say. We shake hands and he introduces himself as Ray. He drove up from New Mexico to buy some horses. Another man stands behind Ray, but I don't see him at first because he's quite short. He introduces himself as Al, Ray's rancher uncle from Saskatchewan.

They ask if I heard them talking about the food. I say, "Yes, and when I heard 'hamburger,' I decided I better let you know that I brought it. You can help yourself to any of the other food, but don't touch my beef!" They laugh, then show me the bread and cheese slices they'd brought for breakfast. I tell them to use my butter in the morning if they want.

I open a can of soup, dish it into a bowl, and put it in the microwave. Al and Ray settle themselves into the chairs at the table. I lean against the counter. We swap stories while I eat.

I keep tabs on my inner feelings. When I grow tired of the talk, I say goodnight.

I feel good about the way I handle the entire situation. I like my initiative, my staying present with myself, my strong exit. To celebrate, I take myself for a stroll under the frosty stars.

Our old vulnerabilities—the pain from our childhood—can paralyze us. No one was there to protect us when we needed someone bigger, someone with clout, to shield us. It's painful to go back to those times when we were defenseless and unprotected, yet the hurt child within us has a strength to offer us if we can face and acknowledge what happened long ago. In the process of revisiting those incidents in a safe way, the inner child gains a new experience and our ego develops a degree of self-trust. With less need to protect the frightened child inside us, the ego has more energy to navigate the demands of the outer world.

The feelings that arose as I listened to those men in the kitchenette came from childhood: bullying by the male principal of my elementary school, public humiliation by a male music teacher during junior high, scolding by a perfectionistic and harsh choir director in high school. Decades after these incidents, the sound of men's voices exclaiming over my food unleashed the discomfort of those youthful events. I didn't replay any of the memories right then, but I did relive the emotions, especially a deep self-doubt. What do I say? Will I handle this the "right" way? What will *they* think? Should I go and confront my fear, or should I sit here and stay still as a mouse? No one but me would ever know what I chose to do in that moment. Playing it safe offered immediate comfort while stepping up and claiming my food stash would show me that I value myself. I chose to stand my ground, and I felt empowered by doing so.

This situation at the beginning of my second solitude challenged my ego. It/I wanted to stay invisible. However, I made myself vulnerable and took the risk of being seen. Then, using both masculine and feminine energies, I set a boundary in a playful way.

Vulnerability is a quality of the feminine principle in that it invites connection. It is often the characteristic that attracts us to children and pets. They let us see who they are without apology. Their affection toward us is untainted, real. They show their pain, their need for food or stroking and cooing. Such requests call forth a tender response in most humans.

Playfulness, spontaneity, and humour also belong to the feminine way of being. They are a means of getting involved with what's going on, bringing a fresh dimension to what is happening. If they are received by the other person, they bring us into intimacy with the moment, with ourselves, and with each other. A warmth and a flow develop, easing our breath, lightening our heart, energizing our body, often making the moment sparkle.

The morning after I set boundaries around my food, I went into the kitchenette to make myself some breakfast. As I reached for the milk in the fridge, it looked like my package of hamburger was missing. A second later, I noticed that Ray and Al had moved it and placed their loaf of bread on top of it so that it looked like my hamburger was gone. I smiled at the joke. We had reached camaraderie. The feminine in me—my playfulness the evening before—had shown up and the masculine responded in kind.

This process of presenting myself to two strange men was a big step toward getting something that had not been present in my childhood. My parents were not able to show themselves to others with clear boundaries; much of who they were remained invisible. Thus, a skill that my ego so badly needed was missing.

Family influences are but one factor in shaping the ego. Another is the sex of the body, which has a significant impact on ego development. Each sex presents fundamentally different psychological issues.

Every human being, whether male or female, has floated in the protective fluid of a woman's womb; has been fed and sheltered by a woman's body; has been privy to her emotions, her movements, and her voice from inside her body. Then, the process of birth separated our body from our mother's. This was a shock, no matter how it happened—naturally or otherwise.

At first, we all still had some familiarity to where we came from. Our mother's smell clung to us. Her voice resonated with us. As we move through childhood and adolescence, though, these shared experiences start to diverge along the lines of our bodies' sex. Girls and boys begin to experience this mother-body in varying ways. For a boy, his mother's body becomes foreign. It is different from his. He is not like her. This is another blow after the trauma of birth. If he is not like her, then who is he?

To answer that question, he has to begin to separate from her psychologically. His identity goes through a spell of "I am not..." In order to come to grips with himself, he needs to feel that his difference from her is good. To fend off feeling threatened by her, or to soothe the guilt he feels around leaving her, he may convince himself that the ways in which he is unlike her are superior.

When the culture around him shuns the feminine, the boy, now moving into manhood, has little to no help in creating a male ego that remains open to the ways of the feminine. It is then easy to disparage his emotions and relatedness and sensitivity to timing. Those traits belong to his experience of the feminine; they jeopardize his maleness. He may scapegoat those things, wall himself off from them, when he sees them in himself.

Modern psychological theories grew out of men studying men and assuming that women developed and matured the same way. This meant that women came up "short" in our mastery of the tasks and challenges that were defined by researchers and theorists as indicators of healthy psychological development.

Of course, women go through a completely different experience. This begins in the womb. During fetal development, the female brain circuits for communication, gut feelings, anger suppression, and the reading of emotions grow unabated. After birth, estrogen fuels verbal and emotional growth. Later still, orgasm, childbirth, and lactation trigger the "love hormone" of oxytocin. We are set up hormonally to join, care, respond, and relate. It makes us agreeable. This dynamic is beyond cultural and familial training. It just is.

Recent studies reveal that "fight or flight" are not the only stress responses to a threat. In fact, they are more typical of men than women. This is a function of hormones. Male testosterone fuels aggression and action; female estrogen combines with feel-good chemicals and flips the nurturing switch on. Researchers call this reaction to peril "tend or befriend."

For instance, the cow's hormonal blend of estrogen and oxytocin produces a calming effect. This serves the survival instinct. When a cow is pregnant or nursing, she does not have the agility required for running or the strength needed to fight. Instead, she joins the herd or, if caring for a calf, goes into hiding with her offspring. Her life instinct acts like the instruction on an airplane to put your own oxygen mask on first, then help those who depend on you. In crisis situations, the feminine notices who needs help and responds (tending) or, if alone in the danger, may turn to negotiating with or comforting the potential perpetrator (befriending).

This hormonal triggering of attachment, caring, and communicating may play a part in women not separating ourselves from our childhood, home, or mother as clearly as men do. We are wired to bond. In addition, girls, whether in childhood or adolescence, look at their mothers and see themselves. Her mother is who she will grow into, and then she does. She develops breasts, has periods. Her voice stays feminine. Girls seem to not have the same psychological need as boys to separate from the woman who grew her in the womb and whose body retains a link to hers. Her father—the foreigner—hangs around and interacts with her, but he does not threaten the similarities between her body and the one that cradled her before and after birth. There was no early-childhood awakening to the innate differences between her body and her mother's; she did not have to transfer her psychological identity from one parent to the other.

Being female, we are not confronted with the direct experience of difference until around age eleven or twelve. At this time, our emotional awareness of life outside family and home expands; it's like we wake up to ourselves in relation to the larger world. Formal evaluations of our ability to focus, perform, think logically, organize, and discipline ourselves come into play. These critiques are more objective than relational. Our skills in connecting, getting along, and cooperating are no longer enough. Our natural way of expressing ourselves comes under scrutiny. An intuitive understanding of a math problem is not sufficient; it must be worked out on paper in a linear way. Facts override opinions. A game is to be played according to the rules and won, not merely enjoyed.

It is at this point that most of us go underground with our truth, which is based on feelings, intuitive thinking, and instincts. We become more reserved, careful to fit in, hesitant to stand out. We do this in order to be part of the group: the classroom, the sports team, the larger society.

Around this same time, we have our first menstrual period and the budding of breasts. Ironically, for many of us, this reinforcement of bodily similarity to our mothers collides with feelings of embarrassment about her. Our body and our world are changing. Mother has been safe but now becomes undesirable, less approachable. Suddenly, we have feelings that seem too private to tell her. Our identification with her makes us uneasy; it is coming into question.

Daughters are notoriously hard on their mothers during adolescence. We resist, rebel, lash out. Such confusion and anger seem to be attempts at separating from her. It's like we are saying, "You are not who I am." Perhaps girls are so unsparing with their mothers because an inner wisdom knows that this is the relationship within which they must become separate while also remaining connected. If she can achieve a sense of self with her mother, she can be a "self" in any relationship. The girl's psychological task is now one of developing a personal identity.

To complicate matters, the girl's culture values independence and individualism more than attachment and relationship. What is natural to her is not esteemed by her society, so she struggles to know who she is, struggles to stand apart while needing to be connected.

Coming into her own sense of self is not straightforward, nor is it easily understood. Yet we must remember that before all else, we are daughters. Relationships and experiences with our first family carry tremendous weight, and they are core to our survival and development.

A mother's view of her daughter may reflect the mother's experience of herself. My mother gave me clothes for my birthday until I was well into my thirties, and they were always a size too small. Part of a large family, abused by her brother, and not seen or heard, she felt insignificant. Her gifts of undersized clothing showed that, unconsciously, she saw me as small too.

The mother may also unwittingly expect her daughter to repeat her own life. As the youngest in her family, one woman stayed home and cared for her mother until she died. That woman then married and had children. Her youngest child was a girl who, upon becoming an adult, began to feel a subtle pressure to stay close to home and look after her mother as she aged. When this daughter came to see me in her fifties, she said, "Sometimes I feel like I'm living my mother's life."

Our relationship with our mother is most influential, and it is never simple. We have all been let down by our mothers in one way or another. As adults, we may be ambivalent about her or blame her or try to fix her. We may distance ourselves emotionally. These reactions to her show that we have not negotiated our own separateness from her. If we blame her, we have not accepted ourselves. If we fight with her or keep ourselves distant from her, we are reacting to her differentness from us. It is through carving out a clear and authentic self within the mother-daughter relationship that it becomes possible to define a self in other important relationships.

Separating out from our mother does not mean that we have to be different from her. It means that we must focus on our own self: clarify our own needs, define the terms of our own lives, take action on our own behalf. We must let our mother be her own person (no matter how much who she is drives us crazy) and allow ourselves to become our own person as well. With each of these steps, we become less reactive—less emotionally attached, yet more emotionally present.

A belief common to women is that we cannot have both a relationship and a self; that we must give up one or the other. Truth is, we can't have a real partnership without bringing a self into that relationship. Our very first relationship was with our mother, and although we are similar in body, we have our own eyes through which to see, our own ears through which we hear, our own voice with which to speak. In other words, we have our personal perspective on things, our unique experience of the world.

We are not our mother, and we have no responsibility to live her dreams. We do, though, have a responsibility to separate out from her in order to find our individual self—an identity that is ours and ours alone.

It is usually our relationship with our mother that sets us up to succeed or fail in maintaining a sense of "I" within the "we" of a friendship or coupleship. The degree to which we can be clear with her about what we believe, who we are, and where we stand on important matters determines to a large degree the level of intimacy we are able to experience in other relationships.

One of my solitudes occurred after a confrontation with my husband in which I quickly dissolved into tears. Nothing felt resolved. Once settled into my cabin, I picked up my journal and began to explore the strands of my upset.

Solitude – Separation Anxiety

Journal Entry

I often cry when I state my position, and I hate it when I do that. What's going on with me that my anger dissolves so easily into tears?

Anger sets me apart from the other person. Anger creates aloneness because my anger is about me. It's about feeling violated in some way; no one else can feel violated for me. I'm the only one who can experience that for myself. In that way, feeling angry separates me from others.

Acting on my anger makes my separateness obvious. Speaking up for myself sets me apart, leaves me alone with myself. When I take a stand for myself, I experience the loss of connection with the other person. This frightens me, though not as much as it used to—it once paralyzed me.

I felt angry about Steve's lack of consideration for me in our life together. The tears came of their own volition as I talked to him. They surprised me.

As soon as I started crying, the anger retreated. The tears retracted my statement of being separate and alone. They admitted Steve's importance to me. They moved me from the position of an autonomous, stand-alone "I" to a relational, let's-be-together "we."

Steve reached toward me with his hand. He accepted the acquiescence signaled by my tears. My expression of anger kept us at arm's length while my tears of hurt moved us back into a fused relationship. Things "righted" themselves in our day-to-day living.

But things don't feel right to me.

I allowed the deeper issues of our life together to be glossed over when I abdicated my anger through tears. We came back together without addressing the attitudes beneath Steve's behaviour and the concerns behind my anger.

It takes a stable ego to stand by our experience of things with clarity and openness. We have to know our stance and trust it. We have to feel worthy and secure within ourselves. The irony and the difficulty are that while standing up for ourselves requires a firm ego, it is also part of establishing a strong ego. At times, we simply must do it before we feel ready to do it.

The more thoroughly we understand ourselves, the better we can act on our behalf. Knowing our fears, our patterns, and our vulnerabilities decreases defensiveness. Remembering that our hormonal nature makes us agreeable and turns us off to confrontation helps reduce self-judgment. We have less need to over-explain, to argue, even to have our way. Accepting that we are who we are puts a lot to rest. From that place, we do not need to change anyone—not even ourselves.

And so, my journal picked up a different thread in the tangled angst about standing on my own two feet. I asked myself when else I feel the fear that I felt as I stated my anger to Steve.

Solitude – Separation Anxiety (continued)

Journal Entry

I feel it when I choose a creative project and begin pursuing it. As soon as I move from daydreaming about something to working on it, I feel uncomfortable. When I share the project with others, I watch for their nonverbal signals of approval or disapproval. I'm hypersensitive to their expressed responses. If they don't share my enthusiasm for the project, I either go underground with it or abandon it. This is evidence of separation anxiety; I don't like standing alone.

I also feel this kind of fear when I take responsibility for myself. I feel like an entity unto myself, and I feel scared.

When I entered university with the intention of getting a degree (as opposed to taking courses only for personal satisfaction), I came close to quitting many times during the first year. The excuse I used was that we "needed money." We did need money, but I was also afraid that I couldn't measure up at school.

An even bigger fear lay beyond that. What would I do if I did finish school? I would have to make decisions about my life. More options would be open to me. There would be fewer reasons to subjugate myself to my husband. I would have as much earning power as he had. I could make my own way in the world. These thoughts terrified me.

Having my own opinion about something brings with it the experience of being apart from the other person. There was a time when I couldn't decide what I wanted to eat or drink when ordering at a fast-food joint. Choosing Sprite when my husband had Coke left me feeling very vulnerable. If he questioned my choice, I proceeded to doubt it myself and often changed my order.

I feel this fear of being separate when I have a thought that is my own in all its uniqueness. I can become so alarmed by the sense of aloneness accompanying it that I choose not to explore my idea. That choice is unconscious most of the time; the idea literally slips from my mind. If it remains with me, I walk away from it rather than developing it, applying it, testing it. Having an original idea induces such panic that I lose myself in caring for others, tending to domestic life, or immersing myself in other people's theories.

At times, my creative thinking shows itself in my work with clients. So far, however, I've not claimed a viewpoint or understanding of my own and taken it into the world.

With these realizations, I admit to myself that even though I am scared, I do desire greater selfhood. This will involve an inner shift whereby I come to experience myself as separate and distinct while remaining in the family and friendships within which I'm embedded.

I want to learn to maintain an "I" within the "we" of my relationships. I want to be able to bear the discomfort of being separate and still be able to function within the tension it generates. I want my expressions of anger and protest to become not only statements of dignity and self-respect, but also be evidence that I will risk standing alone—even when afraid, even in the face of disapproval or the potential loss of love from others.

It's through the ability to be separate, different, and alone that I will become liberated. When this happens, I'll be free to express anger in response to a violation of my sensibilities, and to express love from a position of equalness and mutual respect.

A truly intimate relationship is one in which we can be who we are, which means being open about ourselves. Intimacy requires relentless self-reflection, honest communication, and a profound respect for differences. It requires the capacity to stay emotionally connected to significant others during anxious times while taking a clear position for self that is based on our values, beliefs, and principles.

Getting to this place presents a huge challenge for some women, myself included. The behaviours required for establishing a stable sense of self rise out of our self-worth. A feeling of worthiness has to come from within, making it possible to act in our own interests. However, validation from the outer world can help foster the development of worth, and this is where difficulties often occur. Our society values the masculine and devalues the feminine, and we develop our sense of deserving, of being good enough and therefore acceptable, based on these opinions. For the most part, the institutions of law, education, religion, and science exclude or dismiss the feminine. They rely heavily on the rational, linear, and logical way of masculine thinking.

It is no small feat for the female ego to withstand societal pressures to do things in a masculine way. Some of us were not able to remain in touch with our feminine nature as we moved through adolescence and into adulthood. Bit by bit, we may have stopped trusting our emotions, impressions, and needs. A neglectful attitude toward ourselves as females happens in small ways that pile up and bury us. With knowledge and dedication, all of this can be reversed.

In order to function in harmony with the rest of the psyche, the female ego must be firmly anchored in its instinctual ground, not in the expectations of the surrounding culture. This means that we give as much weight to the needs of our body and feminine sensibilities as we give to the demands of our status and relationships in the outer world. We must learn to embrace our natural intelligence, which is specifically feminine.

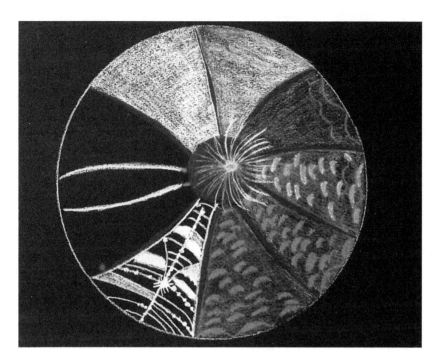

Spider

"By virtue of being in a female body, we women possess an intelligence that, for the most part, remains unacknowledged by our culture. Nevertheless, it exists."
–Peggy Funk Voth

4

Feminine Intelligence

The word "intelligence," which comes from Old French and Latin, stands for "a capacity to understand, comprehend, come to know." The feminine way of coming to know, comprehend, or understand includes instincts, big-picture awareness, and process. It merges with the situation and experiences it. Because of this, feminine time is not made up of minutes, hours, and days like masculine time is, but rather of moments:

- the moment of a child learning to tie her shoelaces (rather than the rush out the door to keep the clock-time of an appointment);
- the moment that culminates in lovemaking (hence the wisdom of foreplay);
- the moment of cooking food that nourishes those who eat it (food does taste better when prepared with full involvement).

These are examples of relational intelligence—smarts that create and maintain relationships. Allowing a child the time to tie her own shoes may look like we're hanging around instead of getting on with things. However, bonding thrives on the active witnessing of a process—being present, attentive, and patient. Foreplay can seem like a waste of time, yet it transforms sex into lovemaking. Food can nourish the soul as well as the body when the cook blends heart and mind with the ingredients.

The merging quality of the feminine brings a round-aboutness to our thinking. Our minds meander around a concept or an issue, looking at it from all sides. In that process of wandering, we discover many tangents that eventually connect to the central topic. Such circular thinking means our attempts to express our thoughts can sometimes come out in a non-linear way. This frustrates others, and sometimes ourselves. It is a problematic way of speaking when we live in a culture based on masculine ways of thinking and communicating—direct and to the point. Women and our ideas are not taken seriously; it is then easy for us to devalue our thoughts and words.

In addition to merging and circling, the abilities of the feminine mind extend beyond those of the brain, delivering a knowing that rises up within our bodies as the "body-brain." It originates in our womb-space—the womb of life, the vessel of the life-force. The womb's wisdom pertains to more than the forming and sheltering of new physical life. It is the home of creativity, of connection with the divine source, of attunement to the flow of life. It knows in ways that the head-brain can't and doesn't.

And it speaks.

I obeyed my body-brain when it urged me to take solitary retreats. I felt a "knowing," a vibration in the core of my torso that told me I needed to do it. As the year unfolded, these times alone began to unsettle my life. My head-brain did not foresee this, and it did not like it.

Three-quarters of the way through the year, my retreat turned into a reckoning of what I have and have not done in my life, ranging from my marriage to my parenting to my vocation. I underwent deep sorrow, with much weeping and journaling. My head-brain was very upset and wanted to do away with my body-brain's sense that all was as it should be. That I needed to wait, to let the realizations settle in.

At the end of the retreat, I physically walked in circles. Though I wasn't aware of it at the time, this mimicked the circular thinking I had done during the solitary days and nights and brought it to a close for the time being.

Solitude – Dragonfly

Before breaking solitude, I go out to the labyrinth mown into a lawn of grass. I feel wrung out, full of fatigue and regret. The slow walk around the circles, leading deeper into the labyrinth, helps still my mind. What will be will be.

I reach the centre and sit down on the tree stump there, facing the birdbath that shines white in the midst of golden flowers. Two butterflies with pieces missing from their wings land on the marigolds before my feet. They stay there, sucking nectar. Their torn wings tremble, and I think of my husband and me. Despite our best intentions, we have hurt each other. My hurting him bothers me the most. Tears run down my cheeks.

After a while, I get to my feet and begin circling away from the centre, widening my way out toward the bigger world. I pause before taking the final step out of the labyrinth.

I am about to return home. Am I ready?

Suddenly a large dragonfly flies straight to my face, hovers, then touches its head to my forehead, right between my eyes. It stays for a few seconds, long enough that I can't imagine it happened. I *know* it happened. The touch feels like a blessing.

Logic and reason suggest that I dismiss this event as mere coincidence, but my body, my feelings, my suffering self all registered it as meaningful—that Nature herself picked up on my distress and offered consolation and reassurance. This feminine "logic," this comprehension, rises out of experiencing the moment.

Women's thinking and communication is often labeled as irrational, illogical, or unreasonable. To me, feminine thinking is *beyond* rational, *beyond* logic, *beyond* reason. It is a different way of thinking that employs something other than masculine objectivity and rationality.

Feminine intelligence includes information that comes from invisible sources such as intuition, insight, sixth sense, reflection, big-picture awareness, and being in the moment. These characteristics come out of a natural sensitivity to life. We live in a state of continuous attunement to our surroundings.

A well-known author once shared that while ironing shirts one day, it occurred to her that she needed a room of her own. This felt like an epiphany. Full of excitement, she shared the insight with her husband, who looked at her blankly and said, "I don't know why you need a room when you have the whole house," then returned to reading the newspaper.

Pondering the incident later that night, the author realized that when she walks into the house, she becomes it. She is instantly aware of all that needs to be done to keep life going. She also realized that when her husband walks into the house, everything and everyone in the house shifts to accommodate him. The children lower the sounds of their ruckus or go downstairs. He puts his jacket where it's convenient to put his jacket—and that's not in the closet. He turns on the radio station he wants. He changes clothes, eats the meal she has prepared, then spreads his work out on the dining room table.

She needed a room of her own. A space of her own. Time of her own. She needed to be able to spread *her* papers, listen to *her* radio program, leave *her* shawl wherever, without anyone else's convenience to consider.

However, even when a woman has a room dedicated to herself and the time to use it, there seems to be an antenna hard-wired into her. She is aware of the sounds in the house—the furnace, the clock, the opening of the lid on the mailbox, the occasional creak. If something is unusual, she knows it at some level. The presence of another person in the house—be it a child, a spouse, a friend, or a service person—causes this awareness to ramp up. Every movement, sniff, sigh, sneeze, flush of the toilet is registered no matter where in the house it occurs. This is common among women; I hear about it all the time in my therapy room. It is also deemed to be the woman's "problem:" she "shouldn't" let these things distract or bother her.

It's not a matter of "letting" them distract her; it's how she is made. This essence of the feminine shows up in Nature.

Solitude – Spider

I notice a spider on my picture window. I place a chair a good distance away from the window and sit down to watch the spider. I peek at it, then look away for a long time, peek again, look away. This is very hard for me—a childhood experience left me with a phobia of spiders—but I repeat the process until I'm able to sit still and watch, my heart keeping a fairly normal beat.

Spider also sits still, a third of the way up the window and a few inches in from the frame. She remains motionless for a long time, letting her food come to her. When she moves, it's with lightning speed. She seems to be able to see with her entire body.

A gnat enters Spider's range of leap and bam! The gnat disappears and Spider curls up, devouring it. Spider didn't crouch before jumping. The single movement she made was the jump.

A big gnat keeps wandering out from the frame of the window and then turns back before it gets within Spider's range of attack. A fly does the same thing. Spider doesn't stir unless something moves close enough. Both the fat gnat and the fly are big. They look like juicy morsels, but Spider doesn't waste her energy on prey that isn't a sure catch. A smart worker, I'd say.

At one point, Spider takes quite a leap, snags her feast, and then freefalls until an invisible silk rope she'd spun and attached to the window catches her.

An inborn awareness of herself and her needs keeps the spider alive. She has within herself all that is necessary for survival: the silk for her web and her anchoring thread; the know-how for creating a web; awareness "genes" passed down by millennia of spiders that inform her shift in attention; and her fine timing for catching a morsel of food.

Women have similar abilities—subtle tunings that have helped the female sex survive all kinds of challenges. We have learned that there is a time to speak aslant, a time to hold our peace, a time to be still and gather information, a time to act, a time to tell our truth. Like the spider, we are able to pick up on things with our whole body— things that are not registered by the five physical senses. This ability is sometimes called woman's sixth sense.

Sixth sense and intuition are often referred to interchangeably, but I want to make a subtle distinction between the two. While both rise up through the body, it seems to me that intuition utilizes the mind while the sixth sense remains on the energetic level.

Intuition is a type of thinking that happens quicker than the logical thought associated with the masculine mind. It gathers information through the five senses, through personal experience, through insight, and through unconscious stirrings. It then connects these pieces of information into an understanding without reasoning them out. Something is comprehended in a flash.

The sixth sense doesn't use the senses of hearing, sight, touch, smell, or taste. In fact, as the name implies, it is another sense in itself that picks up on the energy of a place or person or situation. It is sometimes referred to as "spidey-senses." We know something is off but can't articulate what, nor can we say how we know.

Women are notorious for sensing when their man is keeping secret something that she needs to know. Out of the blue, she asks if his ex is demanding money again. Or, without smelling perfume, without finding a note or a text, without seeing lipstick on his collar or face, she asks her man a probing question about so-and-so or questions if he really has been working late.

A sixth sense can also tell us the truth about something or someone in an instant. This knowing comes unbidden. It does not originate in something we believe or have been told; it is specific to the moment and cannot be backed up by logic or a reasoned argument. For instance, we cancel a trip for no clear reason, just a strong sense that we need to stay home, and a few days later circumstances affirm our decision. Many of us have had the experience of an intense attraction or aversion to a book, person, or opportunity that seemed unfounded at the time but turned out to be trustworthy.

While both men and women are equipped with intuition and the sixth sense, these aptitudes tend to be associated with women more than men. Perhaps women have developed them to a greater degree because of our tendency to focus in a more peripheral and vague way than men do. Or perhaps it has to do with the physical differences between the brains of men and women.

Some recent research claims that the idea of brains being wired according to sex is false. Personal experience tells me otherwise. My husband and sons think, perceive, and remember differently than my daughters-in-law, granddaughters, and I do; the same goes for my father and brothers as compared to my mother, my sister, and me. According to the "myth," which I believe to be true, the male brain is wired front to back with few connectors between the hemispheres. In contrast, female brains are wired side to side, resulting in many connections across hemispheres.

Whatever the reason, intuition and sixth sense inform female thinking. A few years ago, as I was lying in bed reading with my husband beside me, an image appeared in my mind of angels carrying the car our sons were in. It was nighttime. An hour prior, they had left to drive to a town a good hour away to pick up a cousin who was stranded there. I bolted straight up and said, "Something has happened to our boys!" My husband calmly said, "They have a good head on their shoulders; they'll be okay."

Half an hour later, we got a phone call. Along an unfamiliar country road with poor signage, the son who was driving had missed a curve. The car flew across a barbed-wire fence and plowed to a stop in a pasture. Although the front axle was bent, causing the wheels to sprawl outward, our sons found their way out of the pasture and drove to a payphone (this was before cellphones), where they called us. Luckily, one had only a bruised chest and the other a sprained back.

As it turned out, my husband and I were both right. He spoke from a logical and masculine standpoint, me from a feminine, instinctual one.

These two orientations arrive with us at birth and shape the formation of an ego. During childhood, the workings of the mind—taking things apart, comparing, and rearranging—sculpt the male ego, while the deep workings of the psyche—emotions and instincts toward relatedness or connection—fashion the female ego. The feminine way is to relate to instincts, to get to know them without judgment, to learn from them, to listen to them. Often, there is a life-serving smartness to them.

A woman I know, whom I'll call Lisa, acted on this instinctual way of thinking a few years ago. Lisa married a man whose (unconscious) motivation in life was to do as little as he could get away with, while her (unconscious) purpose in life was to emotionally protect the men who were important to her. In her marriage, Lisa kept her irritations and hurts to herself, took care of time-consuming errands, and anticipated her husband's needs. Sheltering him from many of the inconveniences of daily life allowed him to avoid the responsibilities that come with being an adult.

The marriage worked quite well—for a while. But when Lisa reached her thirties, she had two little children and a husband who did not step into his role of financial provider. For more than a decade, Lisa's employment had kept them afloat; now she was not working outside the home. After quitting his job for the umpteenth time, her husband told her that he didn't know where to look anymore, and that she needed to work. A fiery something rose up inside Lisa and, without thought, she said no. "I will not get a job because I'm afraid that if I do, you will never work again."

It felt good for her to say that so clearly and immediately. Later, though, she worried that she might not stick to her position. Her husband had a pattern of passivity, and she had a habit of bailing him out. Between them, there was a practice of him outwaiting her on whatever needed to be done.

Lisa had long wanted to get an education, and suddenly she knew it was time. This was not a logical choice; they had debts, so there was no money for schooling, or even for daily living. Nevertheless, Lisa's body-brain was speaking. This was a belly-knowing, plain and simple. While her head squawked, her belly told her it was time to act on her schooling.

Lisa approached a friend for a loan to pay one semester's tuition, promising to pay him back within a year. After registering for classes, she enrolled her kids in the college's preschool program, which was only available to the children of students. There she recognized several parents from her neighbourhood and offered to drive their children to the preschool along with hers, for a fee. These earnings went toward paying off the loan from her friend.

By dropping her children off every morning and then going to her own classes, Lisa left her husband to stew in his own juices. She always came back to a house in the same messy condition she had left it, but the message about her not rescuing the family financially remained loud and clear.

The neglected house bothered her. However, maintaining her stance about not getting a job was all she could handle at that point, so she didn't address the additional issue of housekeeping. Was she protecting her husband by not insisting that he do the dishes and make the beds while she was at school? Perhaps. But it was a separate issue and pursuing it might have led to her caving in somewhere, somehow. It was a subtle but important choice.

Her ego stood by her, accepted its limitations and preserved its advantage. It was strong enough to defer to her instinctual promptings: the right timing to pursue schooling and the not-right timing to demand more of her husband. This cooperation between ego and instinct interrupted a marriage-long pattern of dysfunction. Lisa changed the dance step in their relationship, putting her husband in the position of having to choose whether he would match her, introduce a new step, or opt out of the dance altogether. Whatever choice her husband made would open the way to a new life.

Although Lisa did not know it, she was carrying out a feature of the maternal instinct. What she did is rarely associated with mothering but is very much part of the whole picture.

To better understand this instinct, let us return to an example from the natural world. The cow instinctually leaves the herd to give birth and remains apart while performing the bonding rituals of sniffing and grooming and feeding her calf. This is the behaviour we typically associate with the maternal instinct. What is not so well known or accepted is the cow's removal of motherly care, which pushes the calf to independence. Once the calf is developed enough to feed and protect itself, the cow gives priority to the call of her own fertility. The calf is no longer the centre of her attention. She leaves it to roam the pasture, joining other cows in heat and working herself into a state that attracts the bull.

The maternal instinct is probably the instinct most commonly associated with women. We usually think of it in terms of a woman's tending of her children: her attention to their needs, her nurturing, her bear-like protection. It gets expressed in her fostering of the home and family life, which may include her husband, pets, and aging parents. In a broader sense, though, the maternal nature encompasses the community—the inclusion of all people and their rights as human beings. It means getting involved with the joys and needs of others, connecting emotionally with those in her presence. It is a sort of merging that attunes a woman to the bigger picture and opens the door to comprehending a situation beyond the obvious facts.

In its full rendering, the instinct surpasses mere caretaking, or even caregiving. It has a tough side. It not only creates a nest in which fragile life can be protected and fed into maturity, but also destroys the nest when it is time for the more developed life to spread its wings and find its own abilities and strength.

An oft-neglected aspect of the maternal instinct is advocacy for our own female needs. It is about knowing when to hand the load over to others out of respect for ourselves. Like the mama bird who rips the weaving of her nest apart or defecates all over it so that it is no longer habitable, the maternal instinct insists that others grow up. Like the cow who abandons her calf when fertility calls, this instinct knows when it is time for the woman to tend to herself.

Many of us come to a point in our lives where our ego needs help to connect more consistently with the deep feminine within ourselves. Years of adapting to the patriarchal expectations of our society weaken the attachment to our feminine knowing we had as girls, and so returning to our native selves often requires a withdrawal from the outer world in some way. Some women go on a solitary road trip. Some leave home for a year. Some take on training for a marathon or another challenge that is their very own. A major illness may introduce a woman to the lifegiving source of the inner world—a steady core inside herself. For me, it was withdrawing into solitude every four weeks for a year.

Solitude – Easter

My bags are packed and sitting by the front door. I dawdle. It's Easter Sunday, and walking out the door feels wrong. The house is filled with a spirit of lightness, fun, happy banter. I enter into the verbal sparring and want in the worst way to unpack my bags and stay home.

I feel like I should be preparing a holiday meal. The ingrained concept of holidays being for the family pokes at me, creating an inner bruise of guilt and longing. Why would any mother abandon her family to be alone while people all over the continent are coming together? What mother in her right mind would walk out the door in the middle of Easter?

Maybe I'm not in my right mind—and that is all the more reason I must go.

I wake at 6:00 to a lightening sky. I dress and start a fire. Tempted to go for a walk, I first step outside to replenish my wood supply. A foot of fresh snow and a north wind greet me, and within moments I'm cold and wet. I decide against a walk.

After being up for a short time, a wave of tiredness hits me. At home I would push through the weariness, but here I allow myself to give in to it. I curl up in front of the woodstove with my head on a cushion and a blanket covering me. I nap for two hours.

It's amazing what a reprieve from the many responsibilities we carry can do for us as women. Getting back in touch with what our bodies need is essential to our well-being, yet honouring those needs tends to be at the bottom of our priority list. There are constant demands on our time and attention, and this keeps us disconnected from our "right minds."

Establishing contact with the eternal feminine rounds out a woman's sense of herself. It puts her ego in accord with the wisdom of her instincts and the rhythms of her body. From that place, she can meet the outer world with confidence, knowing herself to be prepared, ready, and equal as a female.

Contained

"Committing to living fully as a feminine woman exacts a great deal of psychic energy. It also develops courage and meticulous self-knowing."
–Peggy Funk Voth

5

Getting Acquainted with the Feminine

To live in agreement with ourselves, we women need to be friends with our body so that we can receive and benefit from the vague stirrings that rise up through our physical self. We also need to have an ongoing relationship with our internal world of feelings and personal rhythms. Few of us know how to do this; most of our mothers are at a loss. Our culture has no comprehension of the workings of the archetypal feminine—the nature that lives deep within us. Therefore, we have to find our own way to our feminine selves.

There are other cultures who validate the ways of the feminine through practices and rituals. What brought me home to my feminine senses was my year of regular solitary retreats. Through these consistent times alone, I came to know and value myself.

I happened upon the idea of intentional solitudes when a library book I was looking for wasn't on the shelf, but a different one by the same author fell off and landed at my feet. I opened it at random and read about an old healing ritual for women, called a "Healing Quest," which intends to return a woman to harmony with her natural feminine state. (See Appendix A for a fuller description.) A humming sensation started up in my chest, growing stronger as I checked out the book and drove home. The subtle vibration behind my breastbone indicated a body-response, telling me I needed to undertake the practice I had just read about.

I went into solitude thirteen times that year. Dorothy, the owner of

The Robin's Nest where I went for these retreats, had the cabin ready for me each time. She sometimes brought food; she always respected my privacy. I had 160 acres of land outside the city on which to roam, a tiny kitchenette, a picture window, a deck overlooking the mountains, and time on my hands.

Given time and space within a safe environment, the feminine started showing herself. It was quite remarkable, really. I realized that she had been with me, and within me, all along. I had been so busy with my outer life that there was no room for her, with her subtleties of feeling and timing and attentiveness. That changed as my body and psyche came to trust the rhythm of this monthly downtime; the assurance of having three days to unwind, rest, sleep, move leisurely, and let my mind wander settled my entire system. And with that, contents from the underworld—that domain of the feminine—began to surface.

Some of these things were beautiful, but not all were. Long-neglected memories and woundings broke into awareness, bringing to light patterns and truths that busyness had allowed me to ignore. Sometimes I feared going into solitude because I didn't know what would come up or how it would show itself.

Solitude – Rage

My head throbs. I have no Tylenol or Aspirin; I rarely get headaches and therefore don't carry pain-relievers with me. This headache feels different anyway, as if a pill won't touch it.

"This headache feels different . . ."

Fear stabs through me. I had a five-day migraine almost twenty years ago, and I prayed to never have one again. My children were toddlers at the time and my husband was a full-time student. I dragged myself through the first two days of the headache, then called a babysitter who covered the windows of my bedroom with blankets, put a pail beside my bed, and closed the door.

During the next three days alone in that pain-filled darkness, I examined my life. I realized that I was living more out of what others expected of me than out of what brought me joy. I made a deal with God: take away this headache and I will smarten up.

The day that I walked out of my darkened bedroom, I made several phone calls, explaining that I was bowing out of various functions for personal reasons. I didn't know what I wanted to add to my life, but I knew what I needed to subtract.

Two days before going into solitude, I got angry at my husband but didn't tell him about it. I've felt fire coursing in my veins ever since. Arthritis pain stabs my finger joints.

Now, I sit on the couch in my cabin and allow myself to feel my rage. It is as powerful as the contractions of childbirth. It is a migraine, asking me to pay attention. I take the rage and sit it on one end of the couch; I sit on the other. I say to it, "You sit there, I'll sit here. I'll sit with you until you've told me all that you have to tell me."

The first thing that comes is the knowledge that I am unloving toward myself. I'm destroying my body in order to spare Steve's feelings. I avoid conflict with him, but I carry the discord in my muscles and bones and blood.

Yes, that's true. I spare others and slay myself in the sparing. I'm choosing to hurt my physical body rather than tolerate the feelings of aloneness that come with confrontation. I'll swallow my rage and act as if things are fine—smile, have sex, be considerate—rather than risk standing alone in my way of seeing things.

No wonder I've started choking for no reason during the last decade. There's no identifiable pattern to the problem; I can't say that certain foods cause it, or that it happens when I laugh or talk with food in my mouth. But maybe I can't "swallow" my emotions any longer. Refusing to "chew" someone out when I need to shuts off my throat. I am "choking" on my unspoken truth. Because I don't heed my psychological needs, they are being expressed through rebellions of my body.

I nod. This makes sense to me.

I thank my rage and tell it that it's free to go. My head no longer aches. I change out of my nightgown into jeans and a sweater and go for a walk.

I wake once during the night with a headache. I wake again at 6:30 with a severe headache. I drink a glass of water and return to bed. As daylight creeps into the room, my headache worsens. Mid-morning, I draw the curtains closed and light a fire. I sit on the couch, cover myself with blankets, and fall asleep sitting up.

I wake to puke.

My rage is back, assaulting my head. This is going to do me in if something doesn't change. I know that I need to take action when I get home. Yesterday I listened to my rage, but listening without action isn't enough. I have to make some changes. My body is no longer tolerating my abusive attitudes toward myself.

◎◪

Letter to My Sister

I'm realizing how disrespectful I've been toward myself. I've worked hard during the last two decades to change my people-pleasing tendencies, yet there have still been blind spots where I've forced myself to do things I dislike or don't hold meaning for me. The major ways in which I've been unkind to myself are as follows:

- All the times that I've had sex because it was my wifely duty, even when I didn't want it, was too tired, or felt unloved, unknown, or unsupported. I've been told by many people and in many ways that I must meet my husband's sexual needs, but I must look to meet my emotional needs outside my marriage. I'm beginning to question that arrangement.

- The months that I stayed at my last job when the work felt empty to me. I accepted a different position because it paid a bit more and would look good on my resume, but I felt deadened in it. I didn't care about the work. There is little wisdom in doing things that look good externally if they don't bring life internally.

- My marriage is the place where I've been most unloving toward myself. I try so hard to be respectful toward Steve that I end up behaving disrespectfully toward myself. I judge, censor, and deny my needs. I blame myself, try to change myself, expect less of him, make excuses for him, and I end up destroying myself (and maybe us) in the process.

More later, your hurting sister

We women often impose suffering on ourselves by taking responsibility for things that are not ours to take on. We do this by trying to make others happy, by putting up with things the way they are even when they are not good for us, and by staying quiet or at least softening what we say. This is a downside of the feminine tendency to get involved with, to merge with, whomever and whatever is near. Furthermore, this behaviour is also an expectation of our society. We are told to shut up, put up, put out, and get on with things, which is a masculine way of living.

Exposed too early and too long to the weight of patriarchal expectations, few of us are able to withstand the pressure of being measured by male benchmarks. Little by little—or large by large—we abandon our feminine sensibilities. This cripples us.

It is up to us to provide an environment in which we can grow strong and whole. We need a safe container where we can listen to our tiredness, our feelings, our pain; where we can experience ourselves as feminine females; where we can hand ourselves over to our instincts and ponderings; where we can honour our personal rhythms and sink into the ways and wisdom of the natural world.

In her unself-conscious state, the cow is an example of a genuine, untampered-with female creature. She lives outdoors, walks the earth, eats grass, seeks out the shade of a tree, drinks creek water. Her tail swats flies, her hooves and those of her pasture-mates create paths. Somehow, she knows when it is best to huddle with others for safety— usually as a storm approaches. She instinctively knows better than to walk up a cattle chute without resistance.

The cow's body is at one with Nature, resulting in an earthy wisdom. Her knowing comes from an intimate connection with the natural world, and it keeps her alive.

Humans too have a natural kinship with the outdoors. We drink water, eat the earth's fruit, breathe in oxygen, and enliven plants with the carbon dioxide we exhale. Gravity holds us to this planet, and we enjoy the light and warmth of the sun. We gaze at the stars, see images in clouds, splash in the oceans, collect shells, climb mountains, and live with the rain and snow and winds.

In order to truly embrace our femininity, we need to return to being present in that world. It has always been there, with all its feminine abundance and receptivity and healing, waiting for us to see it.

Solitude – Back to Nature

A stack of hand-drawn maps titled "Nature Walk" sits on the mantle above the wood stove. I take one and set out, strolling past an old shed full of antique farm tools. Signs label the tools, telling their use and sometimes their age.

The map guides me into a grove of trembling aspen behind and below my cabin. Sunlight slants between the trees, coaxing gold out of the leaves that carpet the ground. I walk through a gate and into a pasture. I stop before eighty feet of two-by-four planks nailed side-by-side in a zig-zaggy fashion. The map identifies this as the "Homesteaders Bridge" crossing a bog.

The boards bend under my weight as I step onto them. I feel afraid. What if I land in the sea of marsh grasses underneath the bridge? I have no idea what's hidden in there. Snakes? Mud? Swampy water? I don't want to find out. My heart speeds up; balancing on planks has never been my forte.

I make it across the bridge and enter a stand of trees. I walk along—loving the dappled sunlight and the season's smell of fading life—until I sense another presence.

"Hello?" I holler. I see a dark shape moving among the trees downhill from me. Bear? Cougar?!

The beast eases deeper into the shadows as danger fills the grove. Should I run back? Should I walk forward? No one knows that I went on this walk. I wish I'd asked Bill or Dorothy if it was safe to be in this section of their land. They could've told me what to do if I met a bear, a deer, a cougar.

I didn't grow up in this country. I don't know its wildlife.

The creature and I both stand still. Is it looking at me or ignoring me? I can't tell. All I hear is my own breathing. I take one step forward. Then another. Why didn't I talk or sing as I entered this grove? Why didn't I wear some bells?

It turns out to be a cow (I think) with the mangiest, scruffiest, thickest fur I've ever seen. I'm used to the sleek coats of Jerseys; this thing has hair with curls in it.

I get lost. The pasture is dry and the paths have all but disappeared. The grass is short and brown. A mule deer grazes while keeping an eye on me. I see a very large cat with a smallish animal in its mouth. Is it domestic or wild?

I climb over a stile and find a pile of rubble where a house used to be. Not knowing whether I'm still on Bill and Dorothy's land, whether the neighbours are friendly or bristly, I retrace my steps and climb back over the stile, then jump at the sound of a branch snapping near the rubble pile.

Another crack pierces the air. I scurry away from the fence and wander around for a good half hour before getting back on course. When I turn homeward, I see that I have to go back through the woods where the cow-thing scared me and back across the bendy, zig-zaggy Homesteaders Bridge.

I'm glad to arrive back at my cabin.

Once I felt safe, the walk stimulated pleasant memories. As a child, I herded cattle all day without anyone around. I knew the countryside, the wildlife, the cows. I spent enough time outdoors that I was tuned in to its language. I recognized the meaning of the shapes and sounds around me.

Back then, my senses distinguished between the different movements of the grass. I knew whether the rustle was made by the breeze, a snake, a field mouse, a crawling insect, or a cat pouncing. I knew the difference between the chirps of grasshoppers, locusts, and crickets; the cries of bobcats, domestic cats, and cats gone wild; the barks of coyotes and farm dogs. I knew whether a dog's bark meant warning or welcome, pain or fear. The cows that I spent all day with responded to my voice. I called and they came. I led and they followed. I knew their voices and their complaints, and they knew mine.

Now, I'm urbanized. I recognize the difference between a siren and the beep of a truck backing up, but I startle at the sound of breaking twigs. I can distinguish between a police officer, a transit officer, and a security guard, but I fear that a cow might be a bear. I can tell you what band is playing when I hear a song on the radio, but don't ask me to identify a birdsong.

I'm surprised at how easily scared I was today and dismayed by how much I've forgotten.

Disconnection from Nature encourages disconnection from ourselves. We are children of the earth, creatures of an instinctual force. Influences stemming from our sex, race, culture, and family train us to manage our instincts, but they are still there. Hunger, sexual arousal, and menstrual cycles reveal themselves on a biological level; our bodies register these states and respond with stomach growls, plumped-upped genitals, or bloating and blood.

When our emotional responses get triggered, our conscious self—our ego—needs to manage our actions. For instance, we can get grumpy and become verbally snappish if hunger is not eased. Sexual arousal can cause fear or excitement and trigger behaviours that invite or discourage further engagement. Women often feel erotic during ovulation, intolerant during PMS, and energetic and unflappable in between.

In these ways, we are instinctual beings; in these ways, we are similar to animals. Nature is transparent in living out of pure instinct and having a connection to Nature moves us out of our heads and into our bodies. What we bring to the animal nature of our makeup is the human ability to think about what happens to us and what we do. A word we have for that kind of thinking is "rumination." Here the simple cow can once again help us understand what that involves.

While grazing, a cow chews her food only enough to swallow it. When she feels full, she rests. During this time, bits of food are brought back up in a clump—called a cud—for her to chew again. This sounds gross, but it is part of the process through which her body gains nourishment from what she takes in.

Life gives us humans much to digest psychologically. If we do nothing but swallow what comes our way, we gain no nourishment from our experiences and circumstances. Life simply happens to us, and after a while we can no longer "stomach" our lives. We need to bring up the "cud." We need to slow down and chew, really chew, what's been going on in our lives.

When chewing her cud, the cow appears tranquil, peaceful. Her eyes look dreamy and unfocused; the blinking of her eyelashes is slow.

Her whole body seems to be in a deep yet semi-awake repose. This happens several times a day—grazing, then resting and chewing the cud.

Us women need the same rhythm; our bodies say so through their monthly discomfort. If we're listening, our emotions say so through our irritability. We desire to be left alone, to be given space. Our whole being asks us to slow down, to rest, to let our focus relax, let our minds wander. It asks us to be open to whatever enters our awareness. To chew on it, be it an idea or question or problem or memory. Our mental and psychological chewing softens the matter, breaks it down, transforms it into an understanding that feeds us, nourishes us, makes it useful to us.

Solitude – An Internal Vow

Snow falls like a gauzy veil outside my window, making the nearest trees look like apparitions. Birds crowd the trees by my deck, and I watch the seeds in the bird feeders disappear.

I have been wondering about a pattern that has sabotaged me all my life—one that played out earlier in the week as I was facilitating a workshop. Something unexpected came up and I became paralyzed; I couldn't think or speak or act. After people left, my co-leader and I debriefed about the evening. He said, "You are so afraid of doing something wrong that you don't do anything at all." His words rang true.

Now, alone and with no chores or appointments pressing for attention, I lose track of time. Who knows how long I sit before the window, watching the world become smooth and soft and white.

Out of some shrouded place, a memory comes.

I'm taken back to when I was seventeen years old. I'd led the youth group at church for two years, and now it was time for elections. Danny, Roy, and I had all been nominated as Youth Leader. At first, I thought that perhaps I should step down and give one of the others a chance to lead. However, as each of us gave a speech about why we accepted the nomination and what we planned to do in the position, neither of the guys expressed vision or commitment. In fact, they acted like the whole thing was a joke.

I knew that I was dedicated to the group and saw its potential. I was committed to holding regular meetings, preparing for them, and offering quality content. My vision involved inner growth for those who attended, the stimulation of ideas, and the development of a sense of personal spirituality. I believed that if one of the others became leader, the vitality of the group would suffer from a lack of vision. I felt that it would be irresponsible for me to vote for either of them. At the last minute, in a secret ballot, I voted for myself.

By unanimous vote, I was in for another year—which meant that everyone knew I'd voted for myself. My dad, who was sitting beside me when the election results were announced, leaned toward me and hissed in my ear, "Don't *ever* vote for yourself!"

I was stunned and puzzled. Should I have been dishonest when I voted?

Later, as we were driving home with the whole family packed in our little Chevy, he lectured me. "You brought shame to our whole family. You embarrassed me. You're to be humble, not proud. How could you humiliate us with such a show of pride? I can't believe you would vote for yourself. How does that make you, and us, look to the people at church? Don't ever, ever do that again."

I wanted to disappear through the floorboards. I didn't mean to disgrace or embarrass anyone. I hadn't thought about how this would reflect on my family. All my reasons for casting a vote for myself flew out of my head as I promised myself, "I won't, I won't, I won't ever vote for myself again."

I was true to my word; I did not vote for myself again. Not even internally.

After that incident, I learned to second-guess myself. I closed my eyes to my passion and call. I turned away from responsible action and listened instead to an internal voice that boomed, "You have no right…How dare you…"

From there on out, I became more and more invisible in the world and disconnected from myself. I never put myself up for office. When someone nominated me, I made a feeble attempt to disqualify myself. When I was elected to something I wanted to do, I acted as if I was inadequate and undeserving; I didn't admit my interest in the position and its tasks. My behaviours were meant to guard against pride. I believed that it wasn't okay to say, "Yes, I want to do this."

My choice to never again vote for myself constrained my living and shrank my life. I lived without a sense of personal agency; things happen with or without me, but not because of me. I questioned everything I longed to do. I second-guessed every choice I made, large or small. Did I do it right? Could the timing have been better? What did others think? Did I hurt or inconvenience or embarrass anyone by what I did?

In the days that follow, I continue to delve into the effects of this incident. On the last night of solitude, I have a dream that shows me the results of my ruminations and points the way forward. In the dream, I am in a group that meets to share about our lives. I have made a medicine shield, and I go around the circle of people, stopping before each one and saying, "This medicine shield means that I now vote for myself."

To me, the dream I had during this solitude indicated that the inner parts of myself are in support of me voting for myself—of me stepping into the world and claiming who I am. I decided to make a medicine shield when I got home. And I did, but in a modern woman's way, using an embroidery hoop, chamois, leather shoestrings, feathers, and stone-like pendants with little images on them. It hangs on the wall of my personal room as a reminder of this redeemed vow to myself.

When I voted for myself in that long-ago election, I claimed my giftedness and my calling. I saw with an inner eye that I belonged in that position. I had a responsibility to carry the vision for the group and to provide leadership, and in the purity of unquestioned acceptance, I followed the internal guidance that I received.

My father saw my actions but failed to see the motivation behind them. What he didn't recognize was my vision, my sense of responsibility, my *call*. I was sincere in my intentions; pride had nothing to do with it.

Voting for oneself is necessary for living true to ourselves. It occurs in many ways, and they are not always public or visible. A very important arena for self-voting is in establishing a personal balance between Being and Doing.

Hyper-present in our society, Doing is active: learning, getting together with people, planning activities, pursuing achievements and growth in the outer world. It's a time of stimulating ourselves through taking in the world around us. In contrast, Being is beneficial in that we slow down, go inward, and digest and deepen what we have taken in. It is a time of being with ourselves, of reflecting, of dilly-dallying with no goal in mind.

Too much Doing can wear us out; too little Doing can also make us tired. The same goes for Being: too much attention on the inner world makes us weary while too little can be exhausting. Every woman needs to find the rhythm that suits her best. Usually, the challenge is to find enough time and space for Being.

In her pasture, the cow models total acceptance of her need for downtime. She rests several times a day, without guilt, in the midst of her friends and neighbours.

Beyond that daily rhythm of grazing and resting, there is one time when a cow seeks out a secluded spot and the wise farmer does not interfere. That is when she approaches birth. Once the calf is born, the cow immediately sniffs it and licks it, getting to know her baby.

Without this private time and space, bonding does not happen. If other cows are around, they pick up on the birth and come to sniff and lick the calf. As a result, the mother becomes confused and maternal recognition is aborted. She fails to respond to the calf's bleats and does not make her teat available for nursing, nor does she rest with the calf or clean it. The calf becomes an orphan or a communal nursling, feeding from any cow who allows it. The mother wanders and bawls, looking and calling for what she knows she has but cannot find.

The cow taking herself away from the group when delivery is near applies to the labour of birthing our own selves. We need privacy, safety, and uninterrupted time for the process. Given such protection, a new or expanded sense of self can gradually take form. Little by little, we become aware of it as we move about our days and our world. We explore it in privacy, groom it, play with it, discover its skin and scent and contours, all in seclusion as we come to realize that it is born of our suffering. Through this, an intimate familiarity is established. The munchkin-self finds its steady feet, stays close to us. When it is ready, we take it into the public world.

My fledgling, wannabe self—conceived and carried during my year of solitary retreats—had to do with using my voice. I ached to express myself through words, verbal or written. These solitudes gave me a chance to discover, groom, and play with that fragile self.

Solitude – Myself the Poet

One summer morning, I head up to Robin's Lookout. Reaching the crest of the hill, I startle a moose. It looks back over its rump at me, then ambles into the trees.

Cattle have knocked over the bench on the lookout. I gather the concrete blocks and the boards and rebuild the bench. Then I step up onto it and announce that I'll be reading some of my poetry. I invite the flowers, trees, grasses, clouds, birds, mountains, and disappearing moose to listen in. I tell the mosquitoes they can show respect by staying away from the speaker. They obey.

I take a folded paper from my jeans pocket, open it, and read with a strong voice.

A breeze comes through, bending the grasses, tossing the flowers like coloured hats, tapping tree leaves together. I take it as applause, and I bow.

The fertilization, pregnancy, birth, and bonding of my word-crafting self has taken years. Now here I am, writing a book. My sense is that it will soon stand on its own legs and feet. It will soon go into the outer world to meet its own fate.

Women's creative processes mirror the course of physical conception, gestation, and birth. Insights, creativity, and stirrings of inspiration originate within the dark recesses of our own bodies. They do not come to us through our heads; instead, they rise up from inside us. Often, they then drop back down into our womb space, where they nestle while we rush about in the outer world. Later, as we putter in the kitchen or let our focus soften into diffuse awareness while riding the bus, they tiptoe back into our awareness. When this begins to happen more frequently, or when we feel a prevailing discontent, it may be time to look for a place of seclusion. Something wants to be born—wants to come into being, or at least into consciousness. Something that is of us wants to come out and be received. This is a mysterious process, and we often don't know what is trying to be birthed until it appears and we see it for the first time. It may be an understanding, an attitude, a calling. Whatever labours to be born is meant to enlarge our personality. It is meant to bring more of our potential into being.

Talking about our emerging sense of self before it is well-known to us is like exposing the calf to the herd before the mother has internalized its smell: it thrusts the fragile creature upon the mercy of the collective. Others comment on our imagined work of art or the inner change that we sense, and then we no longer recognize it. We feel like something was taken from us, like we lost something. We betrayed the creative nuggets or the urgings toward selfhood that came into our care by showing them to the outer world before they were ready. This happens partly because we don't know better and partly because we ourselves have been abandoned by others. At bottom, we lack a sense of what is our own.

We don't have to keep neglecting what is ours to develop—our unique ideas that come from our bellies and ask to be loved, our real way of being that asks to be accepted and hugged close. We do not have to continue being orphaned from ourselves. One way to bring the internal orphan into foster care is to notice our childish attitudes and feelings, then converse with those sulks and resistances.

Solitude – My Inner Little Girl

Letter to My Sister, Day One

Sis, Dorothy invited me to pick saskatoon berries anywhere I find them on the farm. I silently resist the invitation for two reasons. First, I don't like saskatoons. They're small blueberries. Anyone who grew up with them swears that nothing else tastes like them, but I didn't grow up with them. I've never liked blueberries, and I haven't acquired a taste for saskatoons.

Second, I hate to admit it but there are a few activities from my childhood that I rebel against. Picking fruit of any sort is one of them.

You might remember those awful fruit-picking days. Mom got us all into the car and drove us to some deserted farmyard. Like scavengers, we picked among the trees surrounding a collapsing house. Snakes, spiders, and scorpions overran the place. There was no running water, no washroom available.

Down among the trees, the air clotted with insects, we got bit or covered with little bugs that stuck to our sweaty skin along with dirt and cobwebs and other tree-smidgins. The fruit was small and half-riddled with worms or scarred from hail.

We were stuck there with just a hot sun and the knowledge that we had to keep picking until our mother said we had enough. Oh god, it makes me tired and discouraged to even write this.

No, I definitely don't want to pick saskatoons. Call me lazy, a city girl, or ungrateful—I do not want to pick fruit from its plant. I like the convenience of picking it off the store shelf.

Your little-girl sister

Letter to My Sister, Day Three

Sis, I had to get outside and do something mindless in order to help my brain sort through some issues about money and employment. Usually, I walk while doing this kind of thinking, but the pastures are wet and the road in front of the farm is torn up for repaving. So, I put on a long-sleeved shirt and broad-brimmed hat, grabbed a margarine container, and walked out the door.

The little girl inside me clued in and started throwing a fit.

I said to her, "I know. You did this long ago, far away from here. It was hot, buggy, scratchy, and itchy. You couldn't stop till your mother said so. But today, we're in charge. Let's walk to the end of the driveway and see what the bushes look like. If you don't want to put one berry into our container, that's fine. We'll turn around and come back."

She quieted then.

I got down among the saskatoon bushes, started picking and humming, and lost track of time. When I noticed that my wrist felt tired, I looked down and behold! My dish was full. I felt quite pleased.

I think I have enough berries for a pie. Steve will be thrilled to the bottom of his Manitoba stomach. I promised the little girl inside that she could sprinkle sugar on top of the pie crust.

Your big-girl sister

The parts of ourselves that have been ignored in the past—especially the powerless child-parts—deserve to be given a different experience from what we had as a child. Our inner orphan possesses traits that we need in order to be and feel whole, such as spontaneity and creativity. When seen and acknowledged by our adult-self, the abandoned girl inside opens up, connecting us to the younger self who knew who she was. Through her, we gain access to a youthful zest for life.

One way in which we fail to consider these vulnerable and scared parts of ourselves is by turning a deaf ear to our own needs. As females, we are typically taught that considering ourselves or putting ourselves first is selfish. In truth, if we don't take care of ourselves, someone else becomes obligated to. That is a form of selfishness—it is often unconscious, but it is selfishness nonetheless. Shirking our responsibility for ourselves makes us a burden to others in the long run. We need to be at the heart of our own universe, not at the centre of our children's or spouse's or friends' worlds. Again, the cow shows us something about the feminine nature in terms of nurturing others and ourselves.

In both a human breastfeeding a child and a cow nursing a calf, there is the term "letting down the milk." For cows, this happens when the calf nudges its head against the udder, communicating its hunger. Similarly, a nursing mother can feel the milk release into her breasts when it is her infant's usual time to feed or in response to the baby's behaviour. In both cases, it is an instinctual reaction that comes from deep inside. A similar emotional reaction sometimes happens when we sense someone in need of love, care, bonding, or comfort: we feel a flow of compassion toward the person.

Cultural socialization has exploited this natural spurt of feminine empathy and trained it to benefit others—men in particular. From delivering slippers and a newspaper to the husband when he arrives home to adding a job outside the home on top of the usual "women's work" of housekeeping, cooking, childcare, and carrying the emotional load in our marriages, we have been trained to pay attention to men. We protect them from domestic duties and from their (and our) feelings.

Bless the cow. She not only lets down her milk when the calf is hungry, but she also does so when her udder is painfully full and the farm maiden pulls up the milking stool. This release of milk is for the cow's relief. I liken this to a woman turning her need to nurture toward her own self-nourishment.

Inappropriately providing for others can run us dry. I did this in small ways for most of my life, and over time it depleted me. It sent me into monthly solitudes where, midway through the year, I suddenly noticed one "letting down the milk" habit that often pulled me away from myself.

Solitude – Bill

Letter to My Sister

Snow fell throughout the morning and is still falling, so I've done some deep personal work today. The fog-snow creates a container where I feel safe, as if I can do this work within a protective bubble.

Bill is sweeping snow off my deck and splitting wood for me. His breath makes frosty puffs as he works. Hmmm... an interesting observation occurred to me as I wrote that last sentence.

When I first became aware that someone was sweeping my deck, I assumed it was Dorothy since I'd seen her outside. It was easy to remain focused on my writing, easy to ignore her presence and honour my desire for solitude. However, as soon as I realized that it was Bill sweeping off the deck, I thought that I should open the door to thank him and ask some friendly question. I felt like I should be "nice," that I should acknowledge his presence.

With effort, I squashed the impulse. It's an old training, one that says I must be nice and cheery to men. That I must drop what I'm doing in order to acknowledge them. That I must be available. That a man's presence must take precedence over attendance to myself.

I didn't look up and wave, just kept typing, but his presence did set up a chatter in my head.

Your kicking-the-habit sister

When I noticed that it was Bill sweeping the deck, my socialized conscience had been weakened enough through my solitary retreats that I could stay with myself in what I was doing. Nothing in me felt bad or guilty for ignoring him.

While it is sometimes difficult to resist, the automatic desire to take care of others must, at some point, be put on pause. We need to curb the impulse long enough to check in with ourselves as to who really needs to be the recipient of that mothering energy. A guideline that I have found helpful is, "I will say yes to you only if I am also saying yes to me." My energy needs to be in service to my well-being at least as much as it is available to someone else in their need or desire.

Tending to one's own needs with thought and conscious intent can produce growth. It can strengthen the ground on which we take our stance. It can bring substance to our presence in the world. It can increase our stature. Letting down the milk then expresses its true intent: the fostering of life.

Letting down the milk. Inner timing. Receptivity. Chewing the cud. Who would have thought that the cow could teach us so much through her plain-and-simple animalistic ways?

In her unconscious yet total acceptance of her body and instincts, the cow introduces us to the natural feminine. It is up to us to digest and take into consciousness those feminine properties. Withdrawing from the outer world in a manner that allows us to discover our personal rhythms, to name our woundings, to walk among Earth's creatures, to experience the truth of what we know—this nourishes our entire being. It strengthens our psyche's rootedness in the source of life and delivers an intimate knowledge of ourselves. It brings us home to our feminine nature. It may even transform us into psychological virgins.

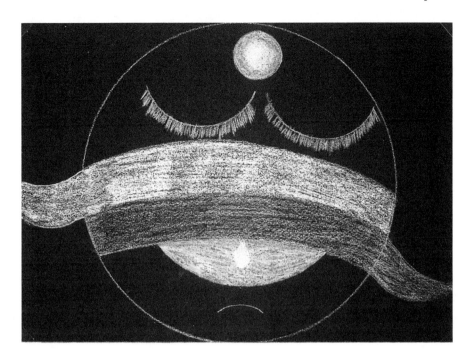

Feminine Eye

"What the feminine brings forth from within us offers a new take on life in the outer world."
–Peggy Funk Voth

6

The Virgin, the Cow, and the Moon

I grew up with experiences of virginity, cows, and the moon that were very different from those of my granddaughters. In my youth, living in a small stucco house in Texas with only a tin roof to deflect the heat, my siblings and I slept outside on army cots in summer. Starlight, breezes, and moon phases lulled us to sleep.

Virginity was protected with diligence. Chaperones attended co-ed events and parents banded together on curfews. There was no pill to prevent pregnancy. Adults and peers viewed virginity as being a gift to be given only as a seal of commitment.

Cows were my companions. They sauntered from the pasture and into the milking barn when I called "C'boss! C'boss!" I told them my joys and sorrows as I milked, their big eyes celebrating or commiserating with me, their milk filling my bucket as I rested my head against their warm belly.

For my granddaughters, milk comes in cartons from a store. They have not tasted unpasteurized milk straight from a cow, nor squirted a stream of warm, white liquid into a cat's mouth. Moonlight is dulled by streetlights, so saying goodnight by the glow of the moon and drifting into sleep with it caressing their face is something they have not yet discovered. The moon remains a scientific fact, not a personal presence. Losing one's virginity is a rite of passage carried out by the uninitiated, unattended by adults and uncontained by marriage. It is something to be given up sooner rather than later—something to be gotten rid of instead of cherished.

There was a time when the deep feminine appeared to us in the mystery of female sexuality, in Nature, and in the faces of the moon. Each erosion of respect and wonder for these things has muddled our ability to see the natural feminine in our modern world. Nevertheless, she is still with us. And when we know what to look for, we can still find her.

The Virgin

Throughout my childhood and early adulthood, the word "virgin" applied only to a woman who had not had sex, meaning that her body had not been penetrated by a man. Today the word is used more loosely, applying to men and women who have not had sexual intercourse.

Centuries ago, the word carried both a literal and philosophical meaning. A Jewish philosopher named Philo of Alexandria lived during the time when Jesus was alive, and he described "virgin" in a way that I find useful. To paraphrase, he said that it is through sexual intercourse with a man that a virgin becomes a woman, but when the divine begins to associate with the inner life of a woman, she is returned to a state of virginity. This may be what was meant by the Immaculate Conception of the Virgin Mary in psychological terms. God, in the form of the Holy Spirit, hovered over Mary, giving her an experience of herself as fully feminine. She in turn gave birth to a novel creature: a human embodying the divine nature.

Through an inner union of opposites—of body and soul, of ego and instinct—Mary conceived a life-giving attitude toward herself in relation to womanhood. She became pregnant with fresh understanding; her life and her place in the world took on meaning, and a state of being whole, of being complete within herself, was born.

Connection with the inner feminine can deliver an experience of oneself as fully woman: a person whose body, psyche, and mind function in harmony with each other. Such a woman senses herself as whole because she *is* whole. She is self-contained, undivided. She is one-unto-herself.

I think an inner initiation into womanhood is especially important for North American women. Many of us have been exposed to women who are powerful in a masculine way; few of us witness women who are powerful in their femininity. It is therefore difficult for us to have an idea of what the feminine looks like and how she operates. It's hard to recognize when she is at work in us or through us, or when she calls us into partnership with her. We need a personal experience that connects us to our own, real, true femininity.

During one of my solitudes, a vision offered me a much-needed connection to the feminine. I was unable to recognize it or take it in at the time, but it was patient and forgiving, returning to me later when I was more capable of receiving the message.

Solitude – The Great She

I nap in the afternoon. When I wake, dusk already swallows the hills, the trees, the deck chairs outside my window. I light candles, feed my fire, sit cross-legged on the couch. I feel peaceful. My breathing slows. For once, my mind sits quiet, as if it too relaxes in a cross-legged, meditative state.

And then, a vision hovers in the air between me and the wood stove.

A massive woman with tanned skin and matted hair intertwined with grass, leaves, and sticks stands in the middle of a cave. There are no features to her face. She is naked. Though she's inside a dark grotto, lush growth and blossoming flowers surround her. She squats and water gushes out of her vagina, creating mist in the cave. Light spurts from her erect nipples, filling the air with soft radiance. Plants take turns feeding on this light, bending their stems so the flowers can suckle at her breasts. I hide behind a bush just outside the cave, watching, afraid to be seen.

I sit motionless on the couch, my breath catching in my

throat, until the vision fades. Then I get up, make supper, do my dishes, and bring in wood. The visitation slides out of my memory.

Two years later, I was ready to receive the vision when it revisited me. This time, my response was different; I was not frightened by the scene, but rather awed and curious. In the vision, I stepped out from behind the bush, stepped just inside the cave entrance. When I sensed that She was aware of my presence, I whispered, "I want to do what you're doing. I want to bring illumination and nourishment to life. Please teach me." As the vision faded, I felt I had been heard.

These encounters that introduce us to our feminine selves are particular to who we are and what we need. One woman described seeing her husband standing nude at the foot of the mattress while she lay naked before him. In a flash, he transformed into a Greek god and she felt the sacred feminine move into her body, filling it, expanding it. Her cells pulsed. The air in the room became radiant, enveloping both her and her husband. This experience left her with a sense of herself as a carrier of the feminine energy, which reaches out to those with whom she interacts.

Another woman felt seen and valued by a male therapist over a two-year period of weekly sessions. The man never touched her or related to her in a sexual way, but when the therapy stopped, she felt fully feminine and experienced herself as moving and speaking with an assurance and a dignity she had never felt before.

A third women shared that her experience came from making brief eye contact with a male stranger as she rode the subway to work. A vibrating energy rose through the soles of her feet and lodged in her chest, flooding her with warmth. Her body felt sensual. Since then, she has become known for her spontaneous and infectious laughter.

Some women connect deeply with their inner feminine through exploring the body of or making love with another woman. It can also happen by the process of a woman coming to know her own body—even making love to herself. Or a vision may bring us to our knees in devotion to the divine feminine. Hildegard of Bingen and other female mystics handed themselves over to the flow of the feminine in and through themselves, producing poetry, songs, and drawings pregnant with sexual and spiritual imagery.

The way in which a woman is opened by the inner feminine is unique to the woman. Whatever form it comes in, it is a gift. It cannot be earned or achieved; if it happens, we are graced. We can only receive it, then cherish it and live it forever. This requires dedication and consciousness while also yielding to the movements of the feminine within ourselves.

The Cow

The cow comes by a state of being one-in-herself without effort. Lacking both dedication and consciousness, her instinctual nature guides her to fulfillment. She is feminine, pure and simple.

In complex ways, the cow holds sway over life in the farmyard through the state of her receptivity. When she is agitated, she roams the pasture, talking to herself, circling her discontent. Then, having enough of that, she joins other restless cows to lubricate herself—to increase her inner heat.

Inside her, the egg ripens. Juices pool, and the egg slides down into them.

The cow stands still, ready for the bull. The climax appears to be submission to the bull, but this seemingly passive readiness to receive ends there. As thousands of restless sperm swarm into the cow's reproductive system, the egg now takes charge, granting or denying entrance to her inner sanctuary. In fact, the unfertilized egg appears to spurn many sperm-cell suitors. Like the cow in whose body she nestles, the egg can be entered only when she is ready, and only by a single sperm that gains her approval.

Many sperm-hopefuls fail to turn her head. She is looking for a tiny one—all sperm are much smaller than she is—that is similar enough to her in terms of sugars and proteins that she senses compatibility.

When she finds the just-so sperm, she opens her door, flutters her eyelashes, and crooks a beckoning finger toward him.

The masculine seed has been whip-tailing, swimming blind and in a hurry. When the egg turns her sights on him, he ups his efforts, takes on speed, propelling himself through the gate, onto the porch, and through the entrance. Once inside, he hears the door click shut and realizes that his energy is spent. The sperm is out of "oomph."

Within the female reproductive system, the lady egg breaks down and dissects both herself and the sperm in order to create something new. The egg chooses essential elements from the sperm to add to her own patterns and makeup. Spooning dollops of enzymes into the mix of sugar and protein, she and he merge into an embryo.

This is the nature of the feminine and of Woman. At a fundamental level, Woman is mysterious. In the inner invisible mystery of her being, she actively dissolves and dismembers what exists in the moment, bringing it into new form.

Woman does this in more ways than producing a physical baby. Every day, she takes in masculine behaviours, activities, and attitudes through her own observations. Every day, she processes them through her feminine ways of understanding. Every day, she creates novel perspectives, fresh routines or rituals, and original environments for the family of coworkers, neighbours, children, and friends.

A woman combines her feminine sensibilities with the efforts of men, and this invisible activity invigorates life.

The Moon

From the cow to the moon, Nature offers us images of the feminine principle in her virginal state. These feminine models uncloak natural patterns within our bodies and psyches as women. All of us—human, animal, and night-orb—live with monthly rhythms.

The moon remains complete within herself no matter the nearness or distance of the sun, the season on Earth, the telescopes pointed at her, or the human lovers making out in her presence. Nothing interferes with her tempo. She follows HER nature, and in doing so, she impacts things within her circle of influence. Her gravitational pull on our planet gives the pulse to ocean tides and steadies Earth's wobble on its axis. Her rounds of birth, death, and rebirth coax the moonflower into bloom, swing human moods, and stir the fluids coursing in a female body.

Women around the world mimic the moon in her various phases as we cycle in and out of fertility, and this is sometimes reflected in our names for menstruation. In some cultures, women call it their "moontime"; others say they are "on the moon." Interestingly, we in North America do not reference the moon at all. My mother's generation called it "the curse" or being "on the rag." Today, we refer to it as "that time of the month" or simply the "period." This lack of moon-connection in our language may reflect our culture's emphasis on science and logic at the expense of Nature and poetry. Nevertheless, our female bodies register the movements of the night's queen.

The moon passes through four phases approximately every twenty-eight days, as do women. Her stages are full moon, waning quarter-moon, new moon, and waxing quarter-moon; our cycle-stages are ovulation, pre-menstrual, menstruation, and post-menstrual.

I have been vaguely aware of the moon's repetitive forms. I have taken her beauty and her mysteriousness for granted; learning about being in a virginal state from her is rather recent for me. As I look back over the insights and events that occurred during my solitary retreats, I notice the sway the moon had on my own experiences, both inner and outer.

Full Moon

A baby girl is born with a lifetime supply of eggs stuffed into two ovary-baskets. At menarche—the onset of womanhood signaled by the first menstrual period—one egg has been nourished to maturity and is released into the slender tunnel of the fallopian tube. This is the first of a female's fertility cycles that will continue for decades.

The egg lingers in the fallopian tube for twenty-four hours. This is the ovulation period of a woman, when the conception of new life is possible. It can be associated with the moon's full stage, when she is ripe and bright in the sky.

During ovulation, a woman typically has lots of energy for outer activities. Creativity surges, bringing enthusiasm, new ideas, and initiative. Sexual desire perks up. Her presence exudes an attitude of receptivity. If she is a waitress, she may notice an increase in tips. If she is married, her husband may observe that she is vital and electric. Mental activity happens with more clarity. Dreams come with more frequency. And so it goes, roughly every twenty-eight days, for years upon years.

And so it has gone—and continues to go—roughly every twenty-eight nights in the sky. The full moon shows up, setting the earth below aglow.

Solitude – Chickadees

On the second night of my solitary retreat, I am visited by a dream. *I'm returning from a walk during a solitary retreat. Pausing on the deck, I look east and see a wizened dwarf-man hidden among the ivy leaves encircling a square wooden pillar. He looks at me and nods. I ask him, "What do I hear?" He whispers, "Chickadees," placing a finger on his lips in a signal to be quiet.*

I am woken from the dream by the radiance of a full moon filtering through the lacey sheers and across my bed. I have the sense that the little man is there just for me, that I'm the only one he would show himself to, and that it's important for me to see him.

As I look for meaning in this dream, I remember an article on chickadees that I read recently. Chickadees don't put on fat reserves for winter like most other birds do. Studies reveal that during autumn, when it's time to store their winter food supply, the memory area of the chickadee's brain is bursting with new cell development. Scientists believe that this proliferation of fresh brain cells helps the chickadee keep track of thousands of hidden food caches.

I am like the chickadee in that I store stuff and remember where it is. The chickadee does that for a season in order to survive through a winter; I, unfortunately, have done it out of a fear that I won't have what I need. I live as if I will never have enough. I am so careful with my pots and pans, my mitts and scarves, my clothing and books that nothing wears out. I save the nice things I've received, storing them away instead of using them.

I have a poverty mindset.

What is this little guy trying to tell me? He hides behind a pillar of vines, which are a form of life: alive, green, and healthy. He is also a dwarf. From childhood stories, dwarves live inside mountains, mining precious ore and stones which they craft into magical swords and priceless jewelry.

Suddenly, I see how my belief that there isn't enough to go around has affected me, not just in terms of possessions but in another area as well. I have hoarded my creative inspirations, stashing them away, afraid that I'll never have another brainchild as good. When the little man in my dream whispered "chickadees," was he hinting that I should return to my stockpiles of creativity, ideas, dreams, and yearnings? Was he telling me to nourish myself by retrieving what I've hidden? Are new connections to memories making it possible for me to recall and recover the contents of those caches?

The dream carries a very personal and intimate quality. It leaves me feeling like I'm holding a secret treasure.

This message from the inner world energized me. I went for a long walk, and as I walked a number of creative ideas that had been abandoned over the years visited me. Some were even linked to current inspirations. It was like my psyche was ovulating, ripe with potential. When I got back to my cabin, I started working on a circle-drawing about abundance. I felt ready to interrupt my hoarding pattern.

Waning Crescent

The full moon and the stage of ovulation burst with life. The next phase of these cycles brings a deflation.

The moon starts to shrink. Bit by bit, day by day, her fullness wanes. The moon declines from full to crescent. She rises smaller each night and disappears sooner. The world is dimmer and seems to grow more still, its objects more hidden as the moon slips away.

A similar process happens with the egg. If the ovum waiting in the fallopian tube is not fertilized during her brief availability, she dies and is absorbed into the woman's body. The womb-nest of nutrient-rich blood, created in preparation for the arrival of that dainty holder of potential life, begins to disintegrate when she does not appear in her fertilized form. This is the pre-menstrual stage.

Like the moon, the woman's energy and mood begin to wane. Routine tasks suit her. She becomes reflective, her attention turning inward as she evaluates what in her circumstances needs to be changed or adjusted.

Some countries treat this female-state as natural and allow space for it. Parts of China and India understand a woman's need for rest and a slower pace, granting her a few days off work each month. In North America, though, society views this time in a woman's cycle as unproductive; it is not a "valuable" time. We are expected to override our need for rest, for downtime. We are pushed to perform without pause. Perhaps this is what causes our moodiness, tears, and snappish behaviour that has become known as "PMSing."

In the manual for diagnosing mental disorders, PMS stands for pre-menstrual syndrome. But it is not a syndrome, disease, or disorder, nor is it an abnormal condition. It is simply a state. I suspect that we would be less difficult to live with at this time of the month if our society made room for our feminine needs. We are not men, and we cannot function like they do without harming ourselves. Yet we live in a society structured by and for men, so we push ourselves despite the fatigue we are experiencing. We force ourselves to focus on tasks when our mind naturally wants to wander. Physical discomfort gets overridden or quieted by pills. We, and our culture, expect us to work and go and do nonstop—like men. This disservice to our female bodies and our feminine selves comes out in negative ways and will continue to do so unless and until our culture accommodates our cycles and the physical conditions that naturally accompany them.

The moon, bless her heart, is not pulled out of orbit by Man's expectations. She decreases without the damage that is done to us in our phase of withdrawal. She models for us a non-negotiable commitment to her rhythms of active visibility and restful invisibility.

This pre-menstrual spell is a psychologically fertile period in that a woman experiences an increase in intuitive knowing. She is most in tune with what isn't working in her life. This unsettling but useful information needs downtime—reflective time—for it to come forward in a useful manner.

Solitude – Unravelling

I feel like I'm plucked out of my earthly existence and set before a judge. My life choices are brought up one by one and paraded before the court. I'm called to the defendant's stand to account for each one. I am judge, jury, and defendant.

My behaviours and activities are placed in a balance and found lacking. Sentencing is delayed, and I'm given a sharp warning to claim my true guidelines for living. I am reminded that I'm on this earth for a purpose. My life will remain unfulfilled if I continue to kowtow to the expectations of others—of my culture or my religious upbringing. If I keep living from a need for approval, I will further diminish my Self.

A whirlpool of grief sucks me under. It surprises me; I feel like I'm drowning. I go under, come up and gulp air, go under again.

Journal Entry

I have to reunite with my Self—with who I am at the core of my being. I can no longer survive apart from it. As I consider this reunion, I witness the unravelling of my marriage.

It's been happening for a long time, this unravelling. In the beginning, what I did was pick up my knitting needles and stitch, purl, stitch, drop a stitch, purl to hold my marriage together. I darned and mended, re-knitting whatever unravelled. I smiled, said sorry, glossed over my needs. I followed wherever my husband went. I supported and soothed, shored up and scraped by. In the process, I got short shrift. Over time, I tired of knitting and put my needles away. Now kinked yarn lies at my feet.

This call to account is delivered by the feminine principle, which is both nurturing and destroying, always in service to the life force. Her natural authority holds a woman to her own abilities and opportunities to advance life.

The archetypal feminine is virgin. She belongs to no (hu)man, cannot be defined or fully predicted. The natural law embodied by the feminine is that of change, as shown by Nature: the seasons, the moon phases, the life cycle of all living things. Chaos, sorrow, suffering, and transformation belong to the feminine.

The feminine side of the human psyche wears different faces. She may show herself as a mother, a wise crone, or a beloved. Her expression may contort into rage. Sometimes she wears the countenance of Death, sometimes that of suffering. But always, these faces appear in service to life—to improve life or open a bigger space for it.

New Moon

Menstruation rids the uterus of the nest that the unfertilized egg did not use. All the materials that went into it—the blood, the fluids, the tissue—are expelled over several days. Emotions settle; tension eases. This is the season of the new moon. The dark moon. The invisible moon.

The woman still looks inward. It is a time of receiving lunar information, vague knowings that stir in the dim depths of life and of the female psyche. There is an urge to move toward change.

In the outer world, a woman may clean her house, her closets, her relationships. As the womb cleanses itself, the woman instinctively wants to rid her life of rubbish, of things that clutter her inner and outer spaces. She is making room for growth of some sort. What has been is destroyed in service to what might be.

All of Nature has its laws, as does our inner world. Just as the law of gravity anchors our bodies to the earth, the feminine principle in the psyche tethers us to our humanness. We are surrounded by her eternal round of birth, life, death, and renewal. Biological cycles, life stages, inner moods, and outer seasons all reflect this rhythm.

The reckoning that I experienced earlier in my year of solitudes came from the feminine. Her confrontation of my small life was painful, yet I trusted her. When my need to give more time and attention to my soul resurfaced in a later retreat, I knew that an honest assessment was not enough. Action was required.

I stayed an extra day at the cabin. Confused and scared about what I was facing, I asked my business partner—a gay, extroverted former priest with heaps of charisma—to come for a conversation about my way forward.

Solitude – Surrender

Blain arrives with his wonderful enthusiasm and realness and transparency. He brings me a CD of African music with a lot of beats and many Nature sounds. I take him out to the labyrinth and the gazebo, show him the cabin on the other side of my kitchen. Immediately, he describes one piece of my dilemma.

He says, "I could see you living in a place like this. One side would be your personal space and the other side would be your work area for seeing clients and small groups. You could be content with living alone and counselling and writing and solitude, couldn't you?"

"Yes, I could," I respond, "and that's part of my problem. I need to write, and I need solitude to do so. My marriage demands a lot of me, and I don't see how I can have both. How I can be a wife and a writer?"

We settle into my cabin and I share with him my present agony in realizing that I am not giving enough priority to my soul—to what energizes me, what gives me a feeling of fulfillment and purpose. I ask him about his process of leaving the church years ago; he clarifies a few things for me, gives me names and words for what I'm going through.

He says, "You're in a place of discernment, Peg. You need to determine what your life must be like in order to be congruent to yourself—your passion and calling—and then ask, 'Where/how does my marriage, job, and family fit into the calling I must pursue?' Clarify first how you have to live and then consider how everything else fits into that."

We talk about my responsibility to my husband. I need to be truthful with him and let him know where my process is taking me, what my vocation and growth require of me. He deserves an opportunity to determine how and if he can live with that. For me to decide by myself to leave the marriage robs him of any say in the matter; it also relieves him of all responsibility in the future of our relationship. That's not fair to either of us.

Journal Entry

Is it possible that my greatest gift—accessing the inner depths through solitude—can also be my greatest seduction? Is my desire to live alone a temptation? Is that drive so strong because solitary work is my destiny in life? Or is my ability to benefit from solitude and self-reflection a personality trait and nothing more? Is it part of my calling but not my total calling?

I love solitude and writing and self-reflection, and I do these things well. They are my joy. Are they to be done to the exclusion of everything else? How do I best give to the world what I have to offer?

Is it possible for my calling to run away with me, rendering my gifts and intentions ineffective? Where is the fine line between stifling it and channeling it into appropriate use? How do I honour my soul-purpose within the reality of my human limitations? The next time I stand before the judge of my life, I want to know that I woke up and honoured my soul-design.

Can my inner hermit and the outer wife be reconciled?

It's a prickly and challenging process for a woman to become one-unto-herself. The moon abides no compromise, nor does the natural law of the feminine energy. Both are impersonal, tending only to their nature, which is what it is: demanding, forgiving, and stunning in myriad ways.

New moon and full moon are both potent phases. The tides of the ocean are at their most drastic; high tides are very high, low tides are very low.

The chickadee dream at full moon brought a profound insight about the wasting of my creative ideas. This new moon trial took me into a deep reflection on the lifestyle I have constructed and what is lacking within it.

Waxing Crescent

At the quarter-moon phases, there is a pause of intensity; Earth's tides are at their least drastic. The moon returns to visibility, a mere wisp of curve that parades larger every night toward its umpteenth debut into fullness. Similarly, the waxing moon of the post-menstrual stage turns our energy and attention outward.

After the menstrual period ends, the ovarian nursery scurries into feeding and coddling another egg into maturity. The womb stocks its supplies for the next egg that will be released into the fertility chute. Cleaned and cleared of all debris, the uterus registers the possibility of new life, anticipating a fresh start.

Psychologically and emotionally, the woman becomes outgoing and upbeat. She expresses herself with renewed confidence and clarity. Enthusiasm takes her into different activities and projects, welcoming fresh ideas. She feels positive in her undertakings. Interactions with others happen with ease.

Life, womb, and house have been emptied and scrubbed to make room for her life, plans, and emotions to expand. The woman's body completes the cycle; she is on an upward swing, and soon she will ovulate.

Solitude – Coyote Song

Letter to My Parents

I'm on another solitary retreat. When I arrived, Bill and Dorothy were working in their yard and called to me to join them. I parked and trotted down the slope to find Dorothy picking mock-orange blossoms and Bill clipping several yellow roses—all of which they gave to me! I am touched.

Returning to my cabin, I saw that the top branches of the dead tree near my deck had snagged the moon sliver. Venus nestled inside the fork of another branch, keeping the moon-slice company. I'll open windows now, take a shower, and hopefully sleep well.

Your twice-blessed daughter

⊙

Before I crawl into bed, Dorothy taps on my door. "I just have to tell you that no one has booked the other cabin. You'll be out here alone again." She pauses for a bit, looking at me with intense eyes. "We never have empty cabins this time of year. You have some kind of power, lady."

After she leaves, I step onto the deck and raise my arms in a stretch. As if on cue, coyotes burst into a yipping song.

These scenes occurred well into my year of solitudes. My consistent retreats and the regular use of the same cabin created a safe place for me and for the feminine. This space and time became sacred.

On an energetic level, I could feel the feminine around me and in me. Obviously, others were affected by her presence as well, including the potential renters of the other cabin who did not come that week and the animals that serenaded me. The feminine principle wields a natural magnetism, influencing those in her sphere much like the moon does.

Women who are connected to their inner feminine have this kind of effect on others. Part of it has to do with the lunar quality of a woman's consciousness. We focus in a diffuse and peripheral way instead of direct and narrow. Our awareness flows rather than staying fixed and is thus able to turn on a dime. We are perceptive in a finely tuned way that leads to a many-faceted comprehension of situations. We see in the dark, so to speak. Monthly rhythms of our bodies teach us to read and navigate life by the light of the moon.

Our twenty-eight-day cycle is divided into two psychological stages: one of reflection and one of activity. Reflection involves the inner world and accompanies the pre-menstrual and menstrual time—the waning quarter-moon and new moon. Activity marks the post-menstrual and ovulation periods—the waxing quarter-moon and full moon. Whether in terms of human fertility or moon phase, each lasts approximately fourteen days.

A psychological rhythm accompanies these physical and orbital rotations. During the two-week period of pre-menstrual and menstrual seasons—of the moon's waning and darkening—the veil between the inner and outer worlds thins. A woman's "sight" moves more easily between her conscious and unconscious lives. She perceives and senses and knows more deeply, more fully.

During the two-week phase of post-menstrual and ovulation times—of the moon waxing into bright visibility—the curtain between the inner and outer worlds drops back into place. Life in the external world resumes its priority. If we trust what we discovered during the weeks of PMS and menstruation, we may now have clarity and motivation to start shifting our lifestyle toward alignment with our individual and womanly priorities.

A cow trusts herself so fully that it's admirable. She doesn't doubt her need for a sheltered place to give birth. She doesn't question whether she should get pregnant or whether her calf is getting enough milk, nor does she wring her hooves over walking away. When Nature calls, she goes, and she trusts her mothering. It's done.

I envy her. She is virgin in that she lives unerringly out of her nature.

As humans, our attitude distinguishes the psychological virgin. When the motive behind a woman's choices is one of coming into right relationship with the feminine principle, her actions are free of vanity and selfishness. This is virginal. Such allegiance fashions a personality of significance and heart.

The state of oneness with oneself attracts others but does not attempt to capture or possess them, does not demand loyalty or expect devotion. Such a woman does not need approval—not even her own. She does not act out of a desire to please or be understood or even to be liked. Being one-unto-herself, the woman does what she does because what she does is true to her perception of things, true to the situation at hand, true to who she is. Though it would be easiest or convenient or even in her "best interests" to say yes, she says no when the inner state of virginity—her body-knowing, the wisdom of her womb-space, her deep inner sensing—requires that she say no. This may mark her as "odd," unconventional, or unusual, but as a psychological virgin, she is not influenced by the societal considerations that cause most of us to trim our sails and go along with the current.

A woman who is dependent on what others think, a woman who says and does things that do not sit right with her, is not one-unto-herself. Shaping one's conduct according to social clichés—how to act in order to be liked or to be a "good" friend, how to behave in order to find a man and get married, how to present oneself on a resume or in a job interview—is not living from a genuine place. Rather than bringing her true and full self to a friendship, marriage, or job, this woman brings her socialized self. She is dependent on someone else's opinions or guidelines for knowing how to live.

All of us are imperfect, and few of us have reached a state of psychological virginity. But the idea of such a virginal condition gives us something to live up to and provides a reason for us to embrace our feminine selves more fully.

Whatever degree of maturity and self-acceptance we've arrived at, each of us brings a unique expression of the feminine and her qualities that benefits the world around us. It is through us as individual women that the feminine finds a home and becomes anchored here. I believe that all of us, whether consciously or unconsciously, ache for the feminine—yearn to feel more feminine.

She longs for us too.

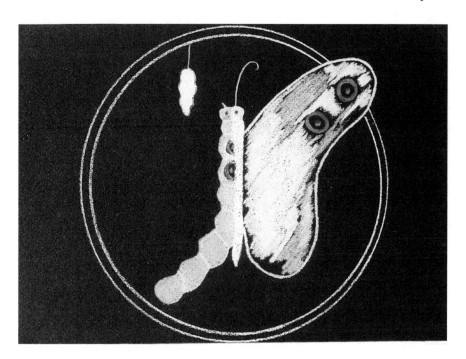

Caterpillar to Butterfly

"By virtue of being female, women embody the feminine whether
we are aware of it or not."
–Peggy Funk Voth

7

The Embodied Feminine

The substance of the archetypal feminine is always with us and in us. Her essence becomes embodied in women naturally, with or without our awareness or permission. Once again, the natural world reveals this truth of native energies and juices; this time, it is shown through the life of a caterpillar.

Solitude – Butterfly

I arrive at the Robin's Nest a bit early for my solitary retreat. As I unload my car, Dorothy invites me to go with her to check on the property of a neighbour who is away. Happy to keep her company, I say yes, and we set off down the road on foot.

Daylight softens as we enter the tree-lined driveway. The air lies still in the groves on either side of our shadowed path. A feeling of enchantment pulls at me and I work to stay present, to keep myself in the here and now.

I notice boxes nailed to some of the tree trunks. They don't look like birdhouses, so I ask Dorothy what they are. She tells me they're for bats. This piece of information shoves me fully into my body; it means there are bats in the area, and I find them a bit creepy.

Dorothy spots a caterpillar on the ground. "Does it have a red or blue stripe running down its side?" she asks. I squat to get a closer look. Then and there, I receive a lesson about Nature that causes a leap in understanding.

"See the blue stripe?" Dorothy points. I nod; it runs along the side of the worm hunching its way across the driveway. "That caterpillar will become a butterfly with blue on the edges of its wings."

"What?! No kidding?"

This truth is so obvious that I wonder why I never made the connection before now. I always knew that the caterpillar holds the fluids it needs for preparing the cocoon and nourishing the embryo inside it. I never understood that it also carries the colours and markings that later become the butterfly's individual designs. *Everything* the caterpillar needs to become its butterfly-self is already there. The worm doesn't become something other than it was; the essence and substance that has been with it all along just takes on a new form.

Crouching beside this caterpillar on a dusky driveway, I realize that I already have within me all that I need to become all I can be. The whole constellation of materials necessary for the complete-me is within me: the dreams, desires, colours, instincts, impulses, character, information, knowledge and drive, along with the ability to learn and evolve. My strengths and weaknesses, my longings and fears, my questions, my weirdness—all are part and parcel of the caterpillar-me that can morph into the butterfly-me, complete with wings, eyespots, and visible colourings.

A caterpillar becoming a butterfly is a feminine affair. The caterpillar spins its cocoon out of the juices of its own body, and then it waits—a necessary stage in the transformation.

The waiting of the feminine is not passive, as it is so often portrayed in tales of women sitting by the window and yearning as they wait for their sailor men to return from sea. Rather, feminine waiting spins a cocoon in which time and space can blend and ripen whatever is at hand. It does not force things, does not put life on hold, does not step out of life. The waiting happens in the midst of life; it is an active waiting that involves being in the moment with an attitude of trust, openness, and receptiveness. It is a complex waiting that takes place in the dark.

A woman-in-waiting holds an inner tension between what is not known and what is before her to do. This combination of alertness and the tending to daily tasks prepares the psychic house for the new arrival. It readies both inner and outer conditions to welcome and integrate a change in outlook or understanding.

Magic happens when the right time arrives; when time expands and finds us, when knowing and timing gel into movement. The topic that wants to be written presents itself. Confusion clears and the way opens before us. An opportunity that presents itself clicks with us. Belly, heart, and head align, and our whole being tells us whether to say yes or no.

Waiting is a hidden activity. Like the caterpillar, generative waiting needs a cocoon, a secure container, and enough time for the transformation to come into fulfillment. It requires time and some form of withdrawal from constant activity. Such patient waiting results in wisdom, which is as delicate, colourful, and free as a butterfly.

The caterpillar-to-butterfly story brought a beautiful "aha" moment to me, and I enjoyed drawing that lesson-of-the-moment after settling into my cabin. But the learnings of the evening were not yet done.

Solitude – The Bat

After watching the sun set, I crawl into bed and read for a few minutes before turning out the light. As I drift into sleep, I hear scrabblings on the wall near the headboard. Are they inside my cabin or outside? Birds sometimes huddle beneath the eaves, so it's not uncommon to hear their movements when I'm in bed. I decide to ignore the rustlings.

As I drift off again, I hear wings hissing through the air. The sound is *inside* my cabin, and it isn't the sound of feathered wings. And then I know. This thing flying in my cabin in the dark is not a bird, it's a bat! I've never seen a bat before, and I don't want to.

Out of bed, on with the lights. I search for him, feeling more anxious than afraid. Where is the creature? What does he look like? Would he come at me if I got too close?

It takes a while for me to spot him. When I do, he looks like a big knot in the wood of the beam that stretches across the apex of the cabin roof.

I spend the next hour trying to get him out of my cabin. I alternate between sitting in the dark, turning lights on and then off, and chasing the bat with a broom. Four times, he flies out the door. Three times, he flies back in. On his fourth exit, I finally get the door closed behind him.

When I calm down enough to think, I remember some things about bats. Once upon a time, in Grade Whatever, I learned that bats respond to vibrations. The bat might've left my cabin sooner if I'd sat still and silent in the dark.

In some respects, my encounter with the bat resembles my experience of the feminine. Bats live in shadowy places while the feminine hovers on the threshold between the inner and outer worlds. Both are comfortable in dim, cave-like environments. The swift and jagged flight of the bat resembles the impulses that flit and flutter at the edges of my awareness. I sometimes recognize the presence of the feminine by a feeling or sense of tiny stirrings on the periphery of my consciousness. These vague disturbances often leave me puzzled, confused, or anxious. Flitting about or hanging from the rafters of my mind, they feel a bit like that bat in my cabin.

I am learning to let these flickers in. The more I pay attention, the more layers I discover. The deeper I listen, the more refined, more subtle, the promptings become.

Giving due attention to these nigglings requires a receptive attitude and an inner stillness that runs contrary to the rational thrust of our society. We have to practice listening and trusting the things that come to us; this is what consciously including the natural feminine is about. No matter how inadequate our attempts at such embodiment may seem to us, the feminine honours our efforts.

One such thing happened for me as I was writing this chapter.

I attended a lecture that was followed by a question-and-answer period. A member of the audience asked a question that I have often pondered. As the speaker began answering, a few thoughts gelled in my mind and I found I had something to say. In fact, I felt *urged* to say what I had to say. How to do that? I couldn't just walk onto the stage and start talking.

Several members of the audience had their hands raised to ask more questions; the moment of addressing this particular topic would soon be gone. Should I stand up and interrupt the speaker with a loud bid for attention? My heart pounded. I wanted to stay in my chair and be quiet, yet the inner prompting refused to be ignored. I had to speak up.

I waited. I knew I needed to speak, but WHEN to speak was not clear. The combination of right action and right timing needed to be there. All I could do was be present to the moment.

And then it happened. The speaker's voice failed.

He took a drink of water and tried to continue talking, but the frog in his throat didn't clear out. The timing was now right. I walked onto the stage, put my hand on the speaker's arm, then turned to the audience and began to speak. This gave me the floor and gave him time to recover.

I have no doubt that because I was open, willing, and listening to the flutterings within, the feminine opened an opportunity for me to act in service to her—in obedience to her promptings.

Since many of the feminine sensings that come to women are deemed "batty," we are tempted to dismiss them. In doing so, we also dismiss ourselves. Taking the time and privacy to give them the respect of honest listening can reward us with a deepening of our inner stability. We become more connected to the feminine within than to the expectations and opinions of the outside world.

As we work on embracing this concept, it helps to know a few other women who are serious about consciously embodying feminine intelligence. Seeking a deeper connection to the feminine can be lonely as so many of us live out of the socialized feminine. We tend to our appearance, our manners, and the nurturing of relationships, but there is more to life. The presence and support of other women who are questioning, exploring, and seeking a fuller experience of womanhood can be helpful.

I have a few friend-companions on my journey of learning to recognize the ways in which the feminine shows up. We are discovering that when we listen, the "knowing" that comes through is timely and split-second. Sometimes, it is even startling.

One of these friends, Susan, experienced an indwelling of the feminine a few years ago as she walked her dog in an off-leash area. She took a familiar path bordered by trees on one side and a grassy area on the other. While she was walking, she noted a disheveled man sitting at a picnic table. He seemed agitated and looked like he had been up all night. Immediately, her "spidey-senses" sent alarms throughout her body. She continued on her way but was now on high alert.

The man soon got up from the picnic table and walked into the trees. Susan's head told her that he probably went to relieve himself. At the same time, she had a hunch to put her dog on the leash, which she did.

After a bit, the man emerged from the bushes and began walking behind her. She could feel his presence. The path narrowed as a large shed for park workers edged up against the pathway, marking the end of the grassy area. Barely into this smaller part of the trail, Susan sensed the stranger approaching fast. An intuitive flash told her to turn around. Upon doing so, she found the man two feet behind her, his arms raised as if starting to reach for her.

Susan did not yell or scream or run. She just stopped.

In Susan's words, this is what happened as she stood facing the stranger: "From the earth, I felt an enormous energy rise up all around and behind me. I felt as if an army of women were standing with me in that instant—an army of women who had been harmed by men in the past. The energy was palpable, like a forcefield, and the message of the forcefield was NO!"

Dropping his arms, the man turned on his heel and hurried away. Susan and her dog resumed their walk and left the park quickly.

The sense of being filled with the vibrancy of the feminine stayed with Susan for several days. She came away from the incident feeling protected and empowered, which moved her into a new level of trust in the messages of the feminine as well as in her ability to listen to them.

What Susan experienced was a feminine form of power. This was not power over the man, nor was it power against him. It simply was power within. This is the feminine way: to stand in the power that rises from within, from a rootedness in the feminine source.

As a young woman, I had no clue that this power could take different shapes. All I knew was power-over, and I exercised it over my body through extreme self-discipline, anorexia, denial of desire, and rejection of whatever made me feel good. Writing this, I feel very sad for my younger self; she wasn't always that way.

During one of my solitudes, I pondered my rebellions. I've been told that when I was two, I threw a temper tantrum that stopped the church service we were attending. Around age three, I liked to crawl underneath the car, make my way to the very middle where no one could reach me, and eat dirt. Stories have it that I taught a cousin to do the same.

My pre-school reputation was one of bossiness.

In my teens, my acting out consisted of driving vehicles faster than was safe. I pushed every car and pickup truck to its limits, bouncing over railroad tracks, drag racing on highways, and peeling rubber on pavement. I also listened to a rock station on a transistor radio hidden under my pillow, shaved my legs against religious orders, and kept a copy of *Peyton Place* beneath my mattress.

Then I married a man who carried enough rebellious attitude for both of us. Together we resisted the conventions of settling down and having a family. We grew our hair long, wore tie-dyed jeans, went barefoot. We hitchhiked, travelled the western US by motorcycle, and lived in communes.

Steve and I did these things together, but he was the one who fielded the criticisms and questions. Our hippy dress and motorcycle interests lay outside the church's comfort zone. Our communal lifestyle left our parents unsure of their place in our lives. Our delay in having children provoked questions and expressions of impatience.

Throughout this era of our marriage, Steve was the shield behind which I stood, quite unscathed, although I was not aware of what I was doing at the time.

In some ways, hiding behind my husband was beneficial. My ego-self was not strong enough to take the criticism or disapproval of others. Nevertheless, what I was unconscious of affected my life. I became more and more invisible to myself. Then I became uncomfortable with being seen by others. I became fearful of life. I didn't know who I was or what I wanted. Without an inner sense of self, I had nothing to guide me, nothing to hang onto when there was no outer pole to which I could tether myself.

It is best not to fault ourselves for what we have been unaware of, yet we must choose not to remain unconscious. When information comes our way that tries to wake us up, we need to wake up. When our bodies speak, we need to listen. When our emotional state disrupts our relationships or our lives in some way, we need to open ourselves to new questions and new insights. When our psyches wreak havoc on us, we need to step back and look at what the chaos is trying to tell us.

These times of regular solitude bring me home to myself. They allow me to get in touch with an internal clarity, an internal authority. My journal receives my ponderings.

Solitude – My Rebellions

Journal Entry

Menopause triggers a deeper, more mature rebellion within me. This is MY rebellion, one not dependent on Steve's participation or protection. One that is claimed solely by me. External approval is losing its grip on my life. Being a good wife, a pretty woman, a responsible worker, a dutiful daughter, or a loving mother is no longer my first priority.

The fulfillment of my own life moves to the top of the list. I'm on a mission to hunt down the meaning of my life. To unearth the person behind the many roles I inhabit. To find room for myself in my life.

My rebellion is an erotic one. I stay in bed until my body wants to rise. I sit and stare into space for wondrous hours. I watch the sun go down. I'm learning to be unhurried when with another person. I covet a slow life, one lived in harmony with Nature's rhythms, and with my own.

The voice of my culture tells me that I'm a fool for slowing down. It tells me that I should work hard and secure my future years. Listening to this advice feeds fear in me. I don't have money put away for retirement. What will happen to me in my old age?

I don't know.

My inner voice counsels me to live according to my personal values and needs. Whatever income I drive myself to make now in service to retirement will be spent on health care in the future if I don't honour my yearning for a slower lifestyle.

Right now, I already have what I require for my later years: stable shelter, a room of my own, a laptop with a printer and small stereo system, a library card, a transit pass, a grocery store within walking distance, meaningful work, friends, children who live their own lives and respect mine, good health, and someone to come home to.

> To the best of my ability, I'll maintain those things.
> Contentment keeps me company when I honour the natural
> pace of my own being.
> This is *my* rebellion.

Because feminine power is so different from masculine power, it can take a long time for a woman to find it, recognize it, and count on it. Coming to that point involves stepping outside the status quo and questioning the typical way of Doing and Being. Within ourselves, we may wonder about our soundness of mind. Outwardly expressing our doubts and perceptions can make us look foolish, even rebellious.

Perhaps this is a form of activism—of active feminism. An activism of Being.

During the times I spent alone with myself, I gradually became aware of power gathering within me. The source of it began to shift away from my external appearance or my habit of being nice. I noticed a down-to-earth quality to it, a steadiness unaffected by outer situations. It's a quiet force, yet it is not weakened by the stillness that characterizes it. This authority is internal and belongs to me, springs from me, resides within me, and exists for me. It is unscripted and free.

One of the seemingly small aspects of my solitudes that contributed to this feminine potency coming forward was sleeping alone. Every four weeks, I left my marital bed and went into a plush, queen-sized bed by myself. There, I learned to take up all the space. There, I sank into my own being without interruption. There, I slept so apart, so separate, that my own rhythms and dreams took on a new clarity.

When we share a bed with someone, our energy fields overlap. This affects our quality of sleep—sometimes for the better, sometimes for the worse. It feels good to snuggle, to spoon into a warm body, to drift into sleep secure in companionship. On the flip side, snoring, nightmares, and expectations for sex can interfere with our own needs around sleep. For women, I believe that periods of sleeping alone can help us settle into our feminine selves and become aware of our creaturely needs, pleasures, and comforts. It can help us embody the feminine more fully.

Embodying something means to express its quality through our body. It means to make something part of one's whole being—to take it in and BE it, carry it in our body, and behave it.

Returning to the nit and grit of the animal world, the cow lives by the natural law of the feminine. Everything about her is feminine—her build, her behaviour, her urges to survive. She gives free rein to her instincts. When she is in heat, it is time to keep life going; she lets her discomfort be known. At the peak of her heat, she allows union. Her egg, upon encountering a sperm, either meets and greets or takes a rain check. In the case of the latter, she returns to her routines, content and comfy as a cow.

During pregnancy, the cow grazes and rests, looking like she's daydreaming. After birth, she licks, smells, and shelters her calf, then lets down her milk and nourishes its bones. She calls it, recognizes it, mothers it, all out of instinct. When that little life is grown up enough to go its own way, the cow has the urge to further life again by reproducing. Off she goes to the salon of other cows that are hot to trot.

The cow has no ego, but we humans do. We are conscious of ourselves, our impulses, and our discomforts. We don't like the suffering that accompanies our bodies for it slows us down. Besides, it hurts.

The female body suffers. It bloats. It cramps. It goes tender to the touch. The flow of life wilts, sending a woman to the couch. She is tired. Her head aches. Her face puffs up, hiding her eyes within fleshy pouches. Her abdomen becomes heavy with the juices of life. Her brain fogs over.

As if that isn't enough, there's the stretching of pregnancy. The monthly strain of expelling the unfertilized egg stops for nine months, but it then swells into the out-of-your-mind labour of birth—followed by stitches, sore and cracking nipples, bloody discharge, and a shrinking uterus. None of it is pleasant or comfortable. Furthermore, sleep and meals are disrupted, bringing problems of their own.

All of that still isn't enough! Next, menopause chugs onto the scene. We flush and want to rip our clothes off, not because we're in heat but because we're on fire and need to be doused. We then wake up in the night to a wet bed and dripping nightgown. The thermostat is broken, and the sprinkler system has a mind of its own. Our skin goes dry and itches. We're miserable enough that sex loses its appeal, at least for a while.

Post-menopause brings the sorrow of bodily losses: the thinning of hair, skin, bones, and vaginal walls. These phases and conditions happen to our bodies in one way or another as we move through the years. A common assumption is that a diminishment of sexuality accompanies these changes, but through my work with women, I find that this is not necessarily so.

We need not lose our sexuality when our cycles stop; in fact, we might move beyond mere genital sex into a full-body sexuality. Like the ripening of grapes or the aging of wine, time can mellow a woman—removing bitterness, adding flavour, turning her tender and smooth. It can bring her home to herself, reveal her worth to herself. These things can make her feel quite sexual. In her body. Embodied.

For a woman, sexuality does not orbit around one or two spots on her body; it includes her whole being. This is true no matter what life-stage she is in: the child-bearing years, pre-menopausal, menopausal, or post-menopausal. Sometimes, though, we may not understand the full-body nature of our sexuality until we are older—until we have the inner security to own the truth of our experience. Often, we are self-conscious about the parts of our body that do not measure up to the ideal shape and size that is presented in the media. When we learn to accept our body as it is, we expand our experience of sex.

At its core, female sexuality is about how a woman feels about her whole self—her personality, her mind, her looks, her abilities. Her body.

Solitude – Sensual

When I wake, I lie in bed for a while, sliding my legs across the smooth tautness of new sheets. I raise my arms and observe their contours, still soft from sleep.

I throw back the covers and lift my legs straight up. They look young and beautiful. I lower my legs, pull my cotton nightgown down, slip my feet back under the covers.

In a few minutes I'll get up, turn the shower on, and let its sprinkles slide down my body until all of me is wet. Then I'll slick myself with liquid soap, lather shampoo into suds, and rinse everything off. While I do these things, I won't think beyond them.

I turn onto my side and stare out the window at the morning clouds. I don't agree with whoever said, "I think, therefore I am." My experience is that I am, therefore I can choose to think. Or not.

I sigh, a soft release of breath, and choose not to think.

Embodying the feminine is about being present with oneself. So much within us threatens to pull us away from ourselves: negative self-talk, self-judgments, a focus on fixing ourselves, striving for perfection, comparing ourselves to others. Being present means just that: being present. Being here in body. No head-chatter, no inner commotion, simply me, myself, and I—female body, the inner feminine, and my ego. All in attendance, all here, right now.

When we embody the feminine, we experience harmony, congruence, and integrity, all of which reproduce themselves in turn. Integrity breeds wholeness—wholeness of presence, wholeness in speech and behaviour—through being at one with oneself. Congruence matches inner and outer; what is inside shows up on the outside. As within, so without. As above, so below. When the student is ready, the teacher appears. Harmony moves up and down the musical scales. Turns discord into accord. Invites union into our lives.

Solitude – Harmony

I sit in front of the big picture window and do my voice exercises for opening and aligning my chakras. At the beginning of my chanting, a doe appears in the meadow beyond the driveway, grazing her way across the pasture and into the trees.

I sing the tone for each chakra three times before moving to the next. After all the tones have been sung, I move up and down the scale of notes, visualizing the colours and feeling the properties of each chakra. The red survival of the root chakra. The orange flow of creativity. The yellow substance of personal power. The healing green of the heart. The blue vibrations of personal expression. Lavender waves ripple between my eyebrows and violet light pulses from the top of my head.

After a big breath and a luxurious stretch, I close my eyes and imagine a root extending from my tail bone into the earth, intertwining itself with the roots of great trees. I visualize a silver antenna extending upward from my head and reaching into the energy vortex of the universe.

As I breathe in, I draw energy from both places—below and above, root and antenna—into my heart. I hold my breath to feel the energy in my heart chakra. I exhale, sending energy back into the air, the ground, the world.

While doing this over and over, I hear my own voice chime, though I'm not using my voice. It peals on and on.

I breathe in and the radiance inside my head brightens. I breathe out and the light in my head dims. And the voice that sounds like my voice goes on. Harmonics ring, fade, rise, as if the universe is responding to my bodily prayer.

When all becomes still and quiet, I open my eyes. The doe is gone. A young buck nibbles his way across the pasture on the other side of the driveway.

It is a feminine sensibility to notice the subtleties of occurrences— like a doe being present at the beginning of my centring exercise and a buck at the end. Like hearing melodious chiming that doesn't exist on earthly levels. Like hearing my voice when I am not using it.

The first—the doe and the buck—can be written off as coincidence. Or, it can be seen as an occasion of both feminine and masculine creatures responding to the aura circulating in my cabin. The aura in my body. As my attention moved from the earthbound colours of the feminine to the colours of masculine heights, female and male animals grazed across the same pasture.

I could say that the second event is impossible, that it is an illusion, that my voice can't be heard when I'm not using it. Or, I can take it in as an experience of joining with, flowing with, elusive energies that can't be seen—a brief encounter of cosmic union.

Embodying the feminine involves being receptive to these kinds of happenings. So many of us saw such things as girls. Sadly, most of us learned to question them and, eventually, to shut them out. But these experiences bring life to life and are therefore worth valuing. They can comfort us and reassure us in ways that staying on a rational level of existence cannot.

Solitude – Celebration

Dusk arrives. I go outside onto the deck. I sit alone. I'm absorbed with myself. I resist all inclination to figure anything out. I let loneliness come to me, and it's a holy companion.

In that melancholic pause when all life waits, poised with bated breath while day tips into night, luminosity reaches its radiant fingers through the air. I breathe it in, and the great mandala of life begins to turn again.

I am alone. I am alive, lonely, and full of life. It feels like a celebration.

Body. Voice. Nature. Stillness. These are the dwelling places of the feminine.

The determination of whether the embodiment of the feminine has a negative or positive effect depends on the attitude of the woman. As a child, I was highly imaginative, spontaneous, and playful.

Unself-conscious. But during my teens, my body and inclinations began to embarrass me. By my twenties, I was a shell of myself. The seven-year depression I experienced in my twenties came from shunning my feminine body and self.

The feminine was with me in my depression, calling me home to her, for she resides in suffering. She is with us in our monthly miseries, uniting us with the eternal cycle of life.

The female body makes it impossible to ignore blood, death, and pain. These bodily conditions give us a natural connection to the feminine side of the human psyche. Our womanly suffering keeps us in life, makes us humble, and kneads compassion into our souls. It leads to endurance. After a lifetime of suffering brought on by no one in particular, but rather by our femaleness, we women know that we can bear things. That we can bear up under things.

All of this produces a feminine strength. A strength of character. A strength of belief in ourselves. It creates a certainty about life and a trust in life.

Over time, these sufferings can produce a contentment that is unshakeable. This kind of surety and peace comes from the feminine source deep within our female psyches and can bring a peaceful surrender to the knowledge that we are both different from and equal to men.

The world needs our feminine ways, which differ from masculine understandings. Many of us are beginning to recognize the importance of our contributions as women—our feminine intelligence, our unique perspectives, our comprehension of the big picture, our feminine empathy and compassion, our devotion to life. The outer battle for equality has existed for a long time, but it is only a part of women's liberation. This fight will not end in the outer world until it expands to the inner world.

It is not men or money or patriarchal endorsement that will make us of equitable value. It is us—we women—who will do this. When we stop trying to be men and instead become real, authentic women, the culture will shift. In valuing our feminine selves, we know our worth.

We experience ourselves as equal, and we act equal. As we embrace our feminine nature in all its contrasts to patriarchal standards and priorities, the masculine power and economic structures take notice.

In the pasture of the cow and bull, new life happens at the timing of the feminine. The masculine wakes up when the feminine enters the ripening part of her cycle.

In North America, the bull was awakened by the feminism of the '60s and '70s. Now, it seems that the collective feminine may be approaching the peak of her fertility. The "Me Too" and "It's Time" movements have the patriarchy sniffing around her, but the bull is threatened. He seems to have forgotten his role in creating new life, and so the scent of the arousing, attracting feminine heat must be strengthened. The feminine needs her herd—the company of full-bodied, full-throated, full-hearted women who carry her essence without apology.

An embodied feminine that is accepted by the female ego brings about a substantial woman whose presence leaves a mark, an impression. It awakens and enlivens both the woman and those who come in contact with her. When a woman receives herself, others receive her.

Embodiment is what makes the inner feminine ready; that inner readiness, in turn, draws forth a masculine response. Not a reaction, which is against something, but a response, which is an openness to something—an attitude of availability.

Beyond all of this, the lovingly embodied feminine invites women to become Woman and men to become Man.

Seedpod

"Without the feminine, the masculine cannot know its
own potency."
–Peggy Funk Voth

8

The Bull

The bull is raw masculinity. His instincts are masculine, his actions are masculine, the way he conducts himself is masculine. Bull nature is ready on arousal; it is demonstrative and directed outwards. In short, it is activity aimed toward whatever attracts its interest.

In Nature, the bull is purely masculine. Bulls are larger than cows; a bull can weigh 2,000 pounds. They may or may not have horns, but they are aggressive. They can go after a person or animal entering their territory, charging with a pounding of hooves, a widening of nostrils, and a focus blind to reason.

When several bulls are in the same pasture, they establish a social hierarchy. Mature bulls dominate younger bulls, always.

When not aroused or challenging for power, the bull grazes, naps, and chews his cud. However, when something catches his attention—be it the farmer coming into his space, the call of another bull, or a whiff of estrus on the breeze—his focus becomes intense, pointed, and primed.

Sometimes bull-talk happens. Growing up on a farm, there were nights when it was hard to sleep because of the snorting and stomping and huffing of all the bulls within a few-mile radius. Most of us had farms of 160 acres with several cows and one bull—that means four bulls on a section of land, each side of that section bordering another section with only a dirt road between them. Within a mile, we could have eight to twelve bulls checking out the competition, calling each other names, announcing their virility.

In terms of breeding, a bull is single-minded and hyperalert.

Witnessing a cow's restlessness, her bawling, her sexual behaviour toward other cows, the bull recognizes that her biological clock is on. He starts checking her out, as if asking, "Is she ready for me?" He watches and waits. He walks near her; he sniffs, he licks.

He keeps checking her out. "Is she ready for me yet?" When the chemistry is there, he butts her hips, nuzzles her buttocks. The cow herself doesn't know she's ready until he approaches her in this different way; his response tells her something about her own readiness. She stands still to receive him, and he mounts her.

Being an animal, the bull has no conscience. To him, heat is heat. He doesn't notice a heifer until she goes into heat, and then she suddenly appears in his line of vision. She has been there all along, but she did not awaken his testosterone-brain until estrogen began to run within her.

Whether the female before him is underage or not is of no concern to the bull. Aroused by heat, the only thing that matters is the object displaying the signs of that delectable estrus.

Sperm is extravagant. Up to a hundred cows can be artificially inseminated from the ejaculate of one bull. No wonder the creature goes mindless—his inner factory pumps out so much semen that his system swells with it. All the blood and brain-presence rushes to the release lever, which is cocked to spill at a dainty signal from a female. Any female.

Upon the release of semen, the bull gives no thought to its future. He just produces more and gives it to whatever will take it.

Psychologically, the behaviours of the bull demonstrate the instinctual drive to directed activity and initiative that the masculine principle brings to the human psyche. Carl Jung defines masculinity as knowing what you want and doing what is necessary to get it. This basic impulse in the masculine element of the psyche may well be at the root of what became a social expectation: that the man asks the woman for a date, that the man sends flowers, that the man buys the ring and proposes marriage. While the inner realm is the sphere of the feminine, the outer territory is that of the masculine.

Some of these societal expectations are beginning to break down;

nevertheless, the custom reveals a truth. The masculine is a doer by nature. Given his drive toward action in the external world, the masculine leads the feminine into the public sphere.

Men fulfill this natural masculine role for a woman in many ways. In my own life, it was my father who launched me out of my childhood home. I didn't realize that I needed to get out of my small town, nor would I have had any clue how to make that happen. But he knew, and he initiated everything from a job to a safe place to live. He drove me down icy roads at midnight to a Greyhound bus stop along a highway, then got my luggage onto the bus and hugged me goodbye. To this day, I am grateful for my dad's sensitive and decisive act of putting me out into the world.

Boyfriends introduced me to roller skating, miniature golf, camping, hot fudge sundaes, pizza, and movie theatres. After marriage, my husband more than once engaged in activities that turned out to be wrong for him but right for me. A male friend of mine, Gary, knew about my dream of getting an education. One day, he showed me around a university campus. I could imagine myself there, and a few years later I walked those same sidewalks as a student. My business partner, Blain, opened the door into private practice.

The masculine offers himself to the feminine through initiating and doing. With the bull in the pasture, it is the cow's readiness that determines whether his actions are received or not. A woman's reception of her inner masculine's moves depends on the readiness of her ego.

When a woman is connected to herself—able to accept her personal emotions and rhythms without judgment—the overtures of the internal suitor begin to wake her up to herself on a new level. This signals a potential fertilization of the woman's creative egg, like the blossom on a tree promises fruit.

Solitude – Seedpod

I move furniture to the edges of the cabin and spread all my circle drawings on the floor—about sixty-five of them. I arrange them in the order that they were drawn. I read aloud a few of the journal dialogues I wrote in response to some of them. As I hear my written words take shape in the space around me, a feeling of personal claiming spreads through me. This is my work, my voice.

I leave my drawings on the floor and go for a walk. Outdoors, images surround me, flow through me. A feather catches my eye and I remember that, for me, body and spirit intersect through my writing quill.

A cow chews her cud while pondering my presence. Ah yes, I have the right to take as much time as I need to assimilate the grasses of my experience and turn them into the milk of understanding.

A dog stands at the end of a driveway, watching me. As I pass by, our eyes meet and I glimpse deep mystery—a mixture of love, longing, and sorrow. Is it that all creatures hunger for more light? More consciousness?

My spine prickles; I'm being observed. A crow perches nearby. Its eye beholds me with intelligence; its gaze stirs something resembling purpose and wisdom within me.

When I'm with other people, I question the meanings that I glean from events and interactions. This uncertainty comes from giving the views of others more credence than I give my own. I'm told in many ways—not all of them verbal—that I give too much significance to "insignificant" things. For years, I believed that to be true.

Today, alone with myself, the vibrancy of seeing "into" things beckons to me. It's part of who I am in that core place where my truest self exists in distilled form. Alone with myself, I come home. Alone with myself, I discover an inner house exploding with detail, colour, and sustenance. When I dare to trust myself, the world opens into nuances that can inform and guide me.

Filled with the satisfaction of being in tune with myself, I return to my cabin and prepare lunch. Afterward, I lie down for a nap and dream of a seedpod bursting open, surrounded by a halo of light.

When I wake, I lie still and wonder what keeps me from dispersing my creative seeds into the world. What stands in my way?

The feminine is visionary by nature. Male artists speak of their muses as being feminine, but I have not heard any women speak of a muse. They sometimes acknowledge a partner or friend as spurring them on, but not as a creative source whom they serve. Individual men have taken me into the outer world, yet no man has awakened creative living or creative ideas within me. It's as if Woman's own nature is the source of women's creativity. It rises up from within our body, our belly, our womb-space.

Sometimes an outer man sees the potential in our ideas and suggests or even provides a platform through which to share them. It is the supportive masculine presence—whether inner or outer—that moves feminine creativity into form.

In a woman's psyche, the masculine brings the focus required for discovering and expressing her individual ideas, opinions, and desires. Knowing what she thinks, believes, and wants orients the woman from *within* herself. A positive relationship between the inner masculine and her female ego enables a woman to follow through on what she knows is best for her.

This dynamic leads us to one more task that a woman must tend to: teaching the man within to listen to her. She must befriend him, enlist him, bring him onboard.

I know, it's enough to have to teach the outer man to listen. We shouldn't have to teach the inner one as well, but we do. This means dealing with the patriarchal snorting and huffing that goes on inside our heads. Though the task is difficult, the payoff is huge. The right attitude on the part of that inner male energy makes it possible for a woman's ego to take her into the world as Woman.

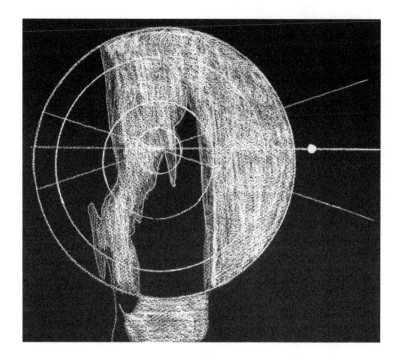

Scolding

"The mighty inner bull must be brought into the service of the
woman's female sensibilities."
–Peggy Funk Voth

9

The Inner Patriarchy

Before I begin, I need to point out that patriarchy is a perversion of the male principle and must not be confused with men. It is a societal structure, not a man, and both men and women suffer from the one-sided and unbounded masculine orientation of our culture. It denies men engagement with their feelings and, among other things, puts unrealistic expectations on them.

A few years back, I stood in the dining room of an old seminary—a school where once only men were admitted. The room was long and narrow, with high ceilings. Hanging just below the ceiling were pictures of great theologians, their faces bordering on scowls, their eyes riveting, evaluating.

These hallowed men had supposedly followed a call from the Divine. Where was the joy?

My husband comes from a lineage of well-known and influential men of a certain church denomination: pastors, ministers, preachers, evangelists. His father carried to the grave the guilt of not having followed in those footsteps. My husband went to seminary, making his parents the proudest I have ever seen them, but Steve was not cut out to be a minister. It has taken him a long time to make peace with that, to shuck from his own shoulders the burden of the unspoken but very present family expectation.

I thought of him, and of my father-in-law, as I stood beneath the severe faces of all those male academics. Their gaze felt judgmental to me. I wondered how it would feel to a man—in particular, how it would feel to my husband.

Women were long denied educational opportunities; perhaps men have long been fenced in as well. Certainly, men in our culture have been denied emotional opportunity. There is little in our society that supports a man in relating to his feelings or a woman in accepting her feminine nature.

The human psyche, whether in a male or female body, contains the archetypal masculine energy. Jung called the masculine aspect of a woman's psyche her "animus."

The masculine principle is associated with the mind. Therefore, the activity of the animus happens in a woman's mind, delivering either a crippling or creative word. According to Jung—and my experience bears this out—a woman's animus adopts the attitudes and opinions of her culture.

Any woman who grew up in North America has developed an internal patriarchy. This is her "bull." It bullies her every day, lashing her with a bullwhip. It enters her china shop, oblivious to the breakage it leaves behind—slivers and shards of her delicate sensibilities, her receptiveness and perceptiveness, her discernments and exquisite knowings. It damages her intuitions, instincts, and empathies, along with her natural knack for relatedness.

When untamed, the inner bull applies the values and evaluations of the surrounding patriarchy to the woman. Her mind-chatter then belittles her. She is too much of this and that, yet she is also not enough. There is always something wrong with her: how she looks or smells is gross, her assessments of things don't make sense, who does she think she is anyway?

One destructive aspect of the inner bull, or animus, is the way in which he most torments a woman. He tells her that she is no good. Then, when someone in outer life—her boss, her husband, her therapist—criticizes her, this judgmental animus is unwittingly fed and reinforced. It's like there is an internal bullhorn that takes up the comment and amplifies it. From there, the negative self-talk spins into half-truths and no-truths. The voice of the animus speaks with authority, offering a barrage of opinions.

Maintaining a personal standpoint becomes particularly difficult for a woman when criticism from the outer world joins with the demeaning inner messages fed to her by the animus. Over time, this animus becomes like the full-grown, hefty bull who, without conscience, mounts a heifer that is too young and undeveloped to bear his weight.

Psychologically, a woman's standpoint collapses under the load of these condemning animus messages; her female ego cannot support itself beneath the crushing burden of inner criticisms. She becomes crippled by self-doubt, unable to rise up and stand by her convictions, her creative essence, her feminine intelligence. This can have a devastating effect.

The evening before I went into one of my solitudes, my business partner and I facilitated a group that involved teaching, sharing, and experiential exercises. The evening was tough for me. I shut down, unable to tie my thoughts together. My mind froze and my voice thinned to a stumbling halt. The longer I was silent, the smaller and more invisible I felt.

Afterward, as I drove to my cabin, I felt weary and disappointed in myself. Why is it so hard for me to have a presence? To feel like I am an entity in my own right? How do I get pulled away from myself over and over again?

The next morning, I dug deep to ferret out what had set me up to feel so inferior that I had psychologically fled the meeting.

The story I recount below casts my husband in a negative light, but he has given me explicit permission to share it. I do so to illustrate how words from an outer man can collude with the attitude of the inner animus to torture a woman. The incident was bad enough, but it was the influence of my *inner* man that did the damage.

Solitude – Shame on You!

Journal Entry

Tears roll down my cheeks; this is the cry of pain. These tears have huddled in my throat for a couple of days. Now that I'm alone, I'm able to let them flow. I'm starting to recognize what made me vulnerable to self-abandonment during last night's workshop.

Last Sunday was the Super Bowl. I baked a large pan of cornbread and Steve cooked up a pot of chili. We took these to a friend's house where we ate while watching the game.

Cornbread was a staple of my childhood, and I love it. On Sunday, I ate a huge piece with real butter and maple syrup. Too full to have chili, I skipped it—an innocent and insignificant choice, or so I thought. As Steve and I drove home after the game, he asked me if I liked the chili he had made. I told him that I hadn't eaten any since I pigged out on cornbread.

He blew up.

After a bit of a rant, he told me I should be ashamed of myself. I replied, "It's a rather minor thing, nothing to be ashamed of really."

With raised voice and a lot of energy, he said, "But *I* made the chili."

"Yes, and I'll have some when I'm hungry later this evening."

"*Shame on you!*" he pronounced. He took one hand off the steering wheel and shook his finger at me. Sparks flew from his eyes and the heat of rage sharpened his voice. "Shame. On. You!"

I began to tremble inside. I said something to deflect his negative words, but I felt wounded.

Later that evening, I did eat a bowl of chili and told Steve that it was good. With a light tone, I made a serious suggestion: "So maybe you can retract your curse of shame."

He didn't respond.

Somehow, that "shame on you" has stayed with me in spite of my efforts to shake it loose. The critical voice of "you can't... you don't deserve...you're not good enough...you have stupid ideas" has hounded me ever since. My internal judge bellows in a loud and insistent voice.

I set my laptop aside, bank the fire, and go for a walk. I feel bad. Inferior. Hopeless. Full of shame. Its presence is palpable and real, making my steps slow and heavy.

Shame on you. Shame on you. Shame. On. You. Shame…

The words pack a wallop. I've experienced them before—I don't remember hearing the words, but I do remember the feelings that come with them. Humiliation. Degradation. Fear. Pain. Shame.

"I'm sorry, I didn't mean to. I won't do it again. I'm sorry. Please tell me it's okay. Sorry."

On the inside, the words pile up into "I'm a sorry human being."

I walk fast. Cold air rips through my lungs while my legs and arms pump. I keep thinking about Steve pronouncing "shame on you." The words attach themselves to me like those sticky yellow aphid-catching strips that I sometimes put into the soil of my houseplants. If that strip sticks to my finger, it leaves a residue, attracting dirt and grit. If it touches a leaf, it can't be gotten off; it sticks so tight that the leaf tears.

The words "shame on you" cling to me like that. They've bonded with my spirit. I can't get rid of the sadness and darkness that I feel.

This is the kind of situation in which a woman's ego must be strong enough to challenge the inner scoldings she receives. It is as imperative that she stand up to the inner man as it is for her to speak her reality to the outer man. The animus must not be allowed to create a bully-squad nor collect negative opinions against us. He must be stood up to.

In the story above, I was able to counter my outer man's scolding to a degree, but confronting my inner man was another matter. His whispers of shame followed me for a week before I had the time to examine my faltering confidence.

Knowing about the animus—that it exists and how it works—makes a difference. Without this knowledge, we can wonder what's wrong with us to make us have these inner condemnations running through our thoughts.

Bull-instinct is simple and direct. Single-minded. Attacking. Bullheaded and pushy. The animus is especially prone to this. Alone and without direction from the female ego, the inner masculine can push a woman to do too much, to ignore her inner timing, to shut down body sensations such as pain and fatigue and grief. She will "push through," telling herself to get a grip, kicking herself for not being able to keep up.

The animus has forgotten its role and taken over.

It is possible for a modern woman to become so masculinized in her behaviours and approach to life that her intuitions and insights struggle to get through. When a woman's ego focuses on developing objective thinking to the exclusion of personal experience and feeling, she is denying her feminine ground. Being only and always task-focused gets things done but lacks the warmth of emotional involvement.

If a woman values competition and winning at the expense of connection and cooperation, she cuts herself off from her feminine wisdom. Pushing her body to perform without regard for its state of fatigue or pregnancy or injury or menstrual cycle robs a woman of the mysteries and miracles that come with being female. Living in such a state of disconnect from our feminine base leaves the female ego confused and leaves the inner masculine alone, unpartnered and without anything to respond to. He then leads the woman further and further from her instinctual nature.

I once had a dream that indicated how masculinized my ego had become. I call it my "Gloria" dream. In this dream, I was outdoors in the country, wearing sturdy boots, jeans, a workman's flannel shirt, and a hard hat. I walked along a path, carrying a pudgy and unattractive bride who looked a lot like the female ogre in "Shrek." But her joy at being held and carried by me—at being claimed as my bride—made her beautiful. Her face glowed with happiness and she burst into song.

"Gloria! Gloria! Gloria!" she sang to the woods and flowers and grass and sky. A breeze caught the edge of her veil, setting it aflutter.

I woke up vaguely disturbed by my manly dress and manner in the dream. I wondered why I was the groom rather than the bride.

As I wrote down the dream, the bride's delight began to eclipse my concerns. She seemed to be so happy at my carrying her that I wondered what it would be like to embrace my feminine self more fully—to carry, or even wed, the inner feminine.

I began to question my masculine orientation toward life. Who would I be without my drivenness to achieve? Without my focus on getting tasks done? On perfection? Who would I be if I wasn't always in a hurry? If I wasn't tired all the time?

Ignoring the body's needs at the behest of a masculine outlook can damage a person. A woman in this predicament is driven to perform, to succeed, to stay on top of everything at home and work and her child's school. She is driven to make holidays and birthdays fun for everyone, to rise at an ungoddessly hour to go to the gym, to have sex rather than making love because she doesn't have the time, energy, or calmness of mind and body to do so.

Our culture values "drive," but it is not for everyone. While it may launch a man into fame and success, it can grind women into the ground through autoimmune illnesses, debilitating PMS, and impossible perfectionism.

The animus, or inner man, tends to dismiss our body-sensations, our sense of timing, and our big-picture comprehensions. This causes us to doubt ourselves. We try to conform to the conventional patterns of non-stop going and doing, of ignoring pain and depression, of pushing through. This can lead us to live so much in the external world that we neglect our inner world. Such disconnection from the feminine realm creates disharmony within us and in our surroundings.

Solitude – Depression

I am tense as I drive into an indigo twilight. A month of ruthless schedules and pounding performance pressures has wound me tight as a clock spring. By the time I reach my cabin at 5:30, I feel battered and fragile.

Bill comes out to meet me. His wholesome face reminds me to breathe—to just take a breath.

The inner spring relaxes a tiny bit. I'm about to enter a place that carries no external demands. I sense that I need to ease into this, to slow down slowly, to let go slowly.

Just take another breath.

Closing the door of my cabin, I let my coat fall onto the floor and drop down beside it. I stretch out on my back, fold my hands across my chest, and stare at the log ceiling. After a while, my breathing slows and steadies and deepens. My mind registers the crackle of the fire. Frequent sighs escape my lips—a typical companion of grief.

I search for my soul, but all seems dead inside. Wooden. No tears, no joy. I do a mental scan of my entire body and find only exhaustion.

In the morning, feeling pull-the-covers-over-my-head depressed and with nothing to get up for, I stay in bed, buried under the blankets. A chill hunkers in the cabin. Outside, the sun shines brighter than my low mood would like.

I turn my back to the window and pray for sleep. It comes in snatches. My body feels like a log, heavy and inert. I'm outside my familiar zone, without any diversion to free me from myself. I'm stranded on an unknown island. Who am I if I'm not working on something? Not *doing*?

At the time I started this year of solitudes, Doing had become an obsession. I truly did not know how to spend my time or how to orient myself without some activity at the centre. Frankly, I knew no other way to be.

During my solitary retreats, I realized that I was addicted to stress and doing. I even displayed withdrawal symptoms common to other addictions: cravings for activity, jittery body sensations, irritability, and mental fixations. There was a time when I knew how to play, how to rest, how to meander without a goal, but I had forgotten how to do these things. I had to relearn them through being alone with myself without distractions—without pressure to go and do and focus.

The nature of the masculine energy within the human psyche is to think with the mind, to take things apart, to analyze, to categorize. Most men can therefore detach themselves from their surroundings more completely and easily than most women can—this level of mental focus and thorough detachment is generally not natural to women. It is feminine nature to combine body and mind, physical and emotional. We bring these things together in our heart, where body converses with mind, where physical and psychological are friends. This weaves a wisdom that enables us to live in a man's world.

One unfortunate choice that many of us have made is adopting patriarchy's glorification of ambition and drive. In this view, it is good to be driven as it shows determination, discipline, and stamina. Being ambitious is honourable; such enterprise, such get-up-and-go, promises a bright future.

These qualities are associated with and natural to the masculine. In their place, they are good traits. Our civilization has made tremendous strides in architecture, technology, science, sports, production, and space exploration because of the masculine features of initiative and single-minded focus.

When buildings collapsed during earthquakes, we went to the drawing board and improved our structures so that they could withstand stronger quakes. We brought the world closer together through television, computers, cell phones, internet. Medical interventions have exploded through research and science, keeping us alive and functioning longer than ever. Sports records continue to be surpassed; instruments that measure and record physical performance motivate us to keep pushing beyond what has been achieved. The production of goods becomes ever more efficient. We have been to the moon and now go beyond. A few of us live in space.

All of this is amazing, and it has come about through ambition and drive. We can be proud of that—of our collective achievements. Like the bull, we have focused, concentrated, refused to be deterred or distracted. We have pursued our objects of desire, penetrated them, and been virile enough to fertilize. That energy is needed to launch things. To push through, push forward, push past. To reach the heights. To achieve our goals. To realize our ambitions.

These are the outer, visible results of single-minded masculine drive. Less visible is the downside of such accomplishments.

Masculine ambition and drive and stamina often asks others to sacrifice all kinds of things in service to its goals and deadlines. Employees may be expected to work inhumane hours or in unhealthy conditions. People are sent into war to protect an empire. Wives and children tiptoe around the house so that the man can concentrate or sleep according to the demands being made upon him. Families are uprooted and relocated. Daily tasks are shifted onto the partner's shoulders while the man hands himself over to his project.

"Behind every great man stands a great woman" could often be more truly stated as, "Behind every great man is a sacrificed woman." Certainly, in all the instances above, feminine values are left out.

Solitude – Stop Pandering

I dream of voices and sensations, no images. I hear my mother talking to another woman. "The one thing I want to tell my girls," she says, "is to stop pandering to their men and live their own lives."

I hear the other woman's voice but can't make out what she says. My mother raises her voice. "They must do it now. It is time."

I say, "But Mother, you pandered to the men in your life."

I feel the blaze of her wrath. "It's *your* life I am speaking of!"

The meaning of the dream seems clear. My internal mother

urges me to step out of old roles, strip away hindrances, and live from my true nature—no matter what responsibilities I carry, no matter what others think. My outward focus needs to shift to an inward one. I need to turn my nurturing and protecting toward myself.

The animus can lead us into activities and commitments that drain us because they are wrong for us. Sometimes it drives us past exhaustion and beyond reason. We and those around us are then robbed of the feminine gifts that lie dormant and unrecognized within the depths of our psyche.

Bringing the animus into the service of our inner feminine means educating it. Being masculine by nature, it knows nothing of the mysterious realm that women's awareness is privy to.

The primary characteristic of the animus is its ability to focus, to shine light on something. It is as if the inner masculine wears a miner's hat with a headlamp. As it moves about the underworld of a woman's unconscious, the beam from its helmet reveals bits and pieces of what is there. When something seems interesting or surprising, the shaft of light hovers on it for a moment.

The animus cannot help itself. It has to focus, and whatever it focuses on comes into its light. A woman therefore brings the animus into service by telling it what to focus on. "Over here!" she must say. "I am trying to understand this. I need your light here."

The animus knows about the mind, about thinking and reasoning, and that's where it operates. But it hasn't a clue about the importance of feelings, which are key to feminine discernment and knowing. Without this knowledge, the animus passes over the feeling element and judges the woman's choices based on what society deems reasonable. A woman must therefore inform the animus about what she feels, the intensity of her feelings, and the significance of the situation, person, or thing toward which she has them. She must be honest about the *facts* of her feelings. She must not be too shy to say, "These are my feelings. This is what is important to me."

For example, a woman's animus tells her that her love affair is shallow, and that it will end soon because that's what happens in love affairs. Or, it may say that she must not trust the man because men only want women for sex so he's going to discard her anyway. It may say that she is a slut. If the affair is with a married man, the animus might call her a marriage-wrecker.

These messages are not helpful. They leave the woman in a muddle.

The animus needs to know about the depth of the woman's feelings for the man, the nature of that particular man, and what the affair means to her. These are relevant details that can help the animus pinpoint its focus. Furthermore, in stating these things the woman begins to define something about herself, which leads to an increased understanding of herself.

Sharing all the data she can about her feelings is critical because of the animus' tendency to flash its light about. His headlamp brings up too many details on the periphery of what she is trying to understand. When this happens, a woman has to say, "No, I don't think that's the point. Please try again." Her feelings will guide her in this. When the animus hits on the right thing, it "clicks." The mind realizes something, and the woman's emotion confirms it.

Solitude – Money Complex

Around noon, I turn to a drawing I've been working on for several months. It's an image representing prosperity—a circle divided into twelve pie wedges. Every wedge is filled with small octagonal shapes. Each slice is a different colour and incorporates the octagonal designs into its individual character. The drawing has taken much time, and a third of it remains unfinished.

I spend three hours colouring it. Detailed and complicated, my intention is that the drawing will remind me that it is possible to experience prosperity, abundance, affluence. It will remind me that those things are possible for *me*. Yet as I colour, instances that reflect a poverty mindset pop into my mind. One causes me to stop colouring and sit back, for it makes my chest hurt.

A few years ago, one of my sons came home from a day of skiing in the mountains. When I asked him if he had enjoyed the day, he said, "It could've been a good day, but I was so worried about getting my money's worth that I skied too hard and too fast and too steady and too long. I wore myself out because I was afraid that I might never have another chance at this."

As I sit with this memory, my mind begins filling with accusations. *You've been a bad mother. You make bad choices. You should have married a better provider. Even your Home Ec teacher gave you a low mark on the paper you had to write about what you wanted in a husband.*

I grab a clean sheet of paper and press my pencil hard into it as I write STOP! STOP! STOP!

I get up and go outside; I need to walk. I swing my arms and take big strides as I talk out loud to that overbearing animus. "I am not a bad mother. Not all of my decisions are wrong. My Home Ec teacher's opinion doesn't matter."

Well, Steve...

"Steve has nothing to do with this," I snap. "This is not about blaming someone. My chest aches when I think about my son being so concerned about getting his money's worth that it took joy from him. That's where I need you to focus."

Ah, says animus. *Never having enough. Might not get a second chance.*

"That's it," I say. "I have lived by those mantras. My son inherited those fears from me." I feel a painful, deep heartache, both for him and for me.

And then I make another connection. A cousin recently pointed out to me that my parents took pride in being poor— that it was part of their identity. At first I was offended, but the comment struck some truth.

As I walk in companionable silence with the animus, my cousin's observation seems more and more spot-on. I feel very sad, both for me and for my parents.

That's a stupid way to live, says animus. *Being proud of being poor.*

"Shush," I say. "That's not the point."

So here you are, the daughter of your parents and the mother of your...

"Yes!" I nod. Here I am in the uncomfortable position between the two generations, a link between the past and present. I am both a receiver and a transmitter of a money complex that limits life. Now that I see this, it is mine to address.

It is desirable that a child surpass their parents in some way. If I can transform my parents' relationship with money—transcend the poverty mindset I inherited—I would leave a trail for my son to even go beyond the headway that I make.

I go back to my cabin, back to finishing my prosperity drawing with its vivid colours and complex design.

When the animus shows us a truth that is ours, that belongs to us, we are stirred. We may even weep, for tears accompany a deepest truth. What is shown may be beautiful or challenging, positive or dismaying. It may come as a memory, a task, a giftedness, an issue; whatever the form, it is ours to develop or resolve, to claim and embrace, if we are moved to do so. My realization that I am a link between past and future attitudes toward money is mine to explore and understand. I may share it with someone else, but it came to me and showed me something about myself. Therefore, it belongs to me. It is mine.

The animus leads a woman to self-knowledge. That is its role. In order to do that, it must be related to rather than ignored or given in to. Its revelations must be received and taken in through our feelings and values. The things the animus shows us must be experienced through our heart and body; only then do they make personal sense.

One way in which the animus takes us to deeper knowledge of

ourselves is through being our student. The animus, in its ignorance about the feminine realm, requires that we communicate what we understand. And as we instruct the animus, we figure ourselves out. We come to know what our feelings are and what our inner stance is.

We women have a burning need to know what we know and trust that knowing. We then have to speak it, for when we express what we know, we know it wholly. From that solid inner place, we can say, "This is my truth. Here I take my stand."

A woman who can say this has neutralized the patriarchy within herself. She does not need to explain, argue, back down, apologize, or even be understood. Secure within herself, trusting herself, and open to life, she is who she is.

In the natural world, the bull does not rule the pasture, the cow does. Her inner timing and fertility reign supreme. Similarly, a woman's inner patriarchy must not rule her pasture. That is unnatural, and it puts the feminine and masculine at odds with each other in both her inner and outer worlds.

The cow's secret to being fully feminine is that she hands herself over to her rhythms. She embraces them, and she busies herself with herself. While in a state of agitation, she does not shoot daggers at the bull with eyes that kill. She does not give him a tongue-lashing. Instead, she walks and ruminates, goes round and round, spiraling in and out of her grievances.

For a woman, restlessness and irritability may accompany PMS or may signal midlife discontent. It is easy to unleash this agitation on others, but to do so is unwise. This releases the tension, but it undermines the purpose of her frustration. If held within herself, dissatisfaction could lead to change or to a deeper self-understanding. Agitation is a time for tending to herself—for paying attention to the truth of her life.

Instead of lashing out, a woman may scrub the floors or shut the door to her office. Her attention needs to be on herself.

When fidgety cows gather, they are not blaming the bull for their discomfort. Instead, they are strengthening their feminine heat in order to meet him in a state of readiness. This corresponds to gatherings of women that generate confidence in our worthiness, enabling us to meet our men and our society from a place rooted in our nature. Though the ground may be uneven, rocky or shifting, we are held steady from within.

Achieving inner equality requires that a woman's female ego accept her feminine sensibilities of timing, receptivity, and emotional relatedness. The inner patriarchy will then no longer rule the pasture; the animus will be managed by feminine timing.

For a woman, the exalted traits of discipline, ambition, and stamina need to be in service to her natural way of being. Self-discipline can serve her well in relation to self-care, allowing her to rest when tired, to meditate or exercise when stressed, to slow the pace of her lifestyle when feeling constantly rushed, to follow process-time rather than clock-time when that's best in the moment.

Ambition benefits a woman when she is clear about what she needs and wants, not what she is supposed to need and want. It motivates her to pursue her aspirations in a way that includes the whole of her life: her relationships, her health, her interests, her intuitions, and her timing.

Stamina helps us stick to something—to see it through to completion. The flexible and inclusive nature of the feminine enables a woman to maintain a single-minded determination on the periphery of tending to the demands of daily life.

Present in both males and females, feminine and masculine orientations are available to all of us—the two sexes simply express them differently. Infused with testosterone or estrogen, these raw energies come forth more clearly in one sex or the other. The same energy also lies in the opposite sex but is exercised in another way.

There are two sculptures in the US that portray this contrast. The first is a statue of a charging bull that stands in the financial district of New York City. It is a beautiful bronze creature with head lowered, nostrils flared, shoulders bulging, legs crouched to move, horns and tail erect. The artist's intent was to symbolize the power and strength of the American people after the stock market crash in 1987. Personally financed, created, and installed by the artist in 1989, it is a personification of alert readiness, the bull's body pumped with adrenaline and revved to go. It is appropriate for a financial district where dogged ambition and aggression are required.

The statue draws tourists. Some touch the horns, supposedly for good luck. Some sit atop the broad, mighty back. Men sometimes stroke its testicle-sac.

On the eve of International Women's Day in 2017, a bronze statue of a young female appeared in front of the bull. Hair in a ponytail, hands on hips, and feet spread in a solid stance, the girl faces the bull, looking him squarely in the eye.

The girl statue was meant to be a reminder of and encouragement toward the inclusion of women in the financial field. Her creator points out that she made the girl's features and posture soft, proud, and brave, not belligerent. The statue of the fearless girl provides a model for correcting patriarchy's imbalance by including the feminine. She displays courage.

The root of the word courage is heart—"coeur" means "heart" in French. The feminine approach is through the heart, be it bravery, strength, or influence that is exercised.

It takes strength of heart to resist without violence. It takes bravery to protest with heart. It takes relatedness to influence from the heart. This is the way to approach the animus, which draws its attitude from the patriarchal culture. A fearless stance toward the patriarchy within ourselves, done with heart, changes us from the inside out. We come home to the feminine. As this shift happens within more and more of us, the outer patriarchy will change too.

Harmony

"When a woman's inner masculine is operating through a stable
female ego, there is no snorting or bellowing or pawing
at the ground."
–Peggy Funk Voth

10

Masculine Responsiveness

In the cow pasture, the bull's muscular activity is both curbed and awakened by the fertility of the female. Without the attraction of her heat, his focus wanders everywhere. Without her engagement, his impregnating abilities find no satisfaction. When received by the cow—which cannot happen willy-nilly, but only in a timely fashion—the bull's stature and offerings can reach fulfillment.

The masculine follows when the feminine is rooted within herself; this is true in both the inner and outer world. Most of my focus here is on the animus, but a point needs to be made about the flesh-and-blood men in our external lives.

Men cannot move about the internal world with the ease that we women can. The inner world is the realm of the feminine; for a woman, a healthy ego is rooted in the instincts and intellect of her interior world. In men, the feminine mediates between the unconscious and their male ego, and so they do not have the first-hand experience of the inner workings that women do. Emotions are not as easily accessible to them. Intuitive flashes do not happen in the same way. Subtle knowings do not rise up from their bellies, for their awarenesses occur in the mind more so than the body. Human men therefore need to be *shown* the feminine way, not talked to about it.

The most timesaving, energy-saving approach to educating a man about the deep feminine is to give him experiences of it. For us women, this means living out of a connection with the feminine. Believing that she exists and is present in us. Accepting ourselves as feminine creatures with rhythms, emotions, and uncanny timing.

Giving a man an experience of the feminine involves relating to him in a non-threatening way—in a way that does not make him feel emasculated or drive him to retreat. He does not need to be lectured, browbeaten, or cowed.

In the life of cattle, bull-calves are sometimes castrated. This is a physical act that takes away the calf's masculinity, making it docile. Some of these neutered calves head to the rodeo for steer-wrestling or steer-roping. Most are raised to be cut into steaks and ground into hamburger. Similarly, men can be castrated emotionally and psychologically by women, turning them into anemic shadows of themselves. Mockery or humiliation of a man may come out of a woman's resentment that he is not what she expects him to be, but they injure his sense of masculinity. This is not life-giving and indicates that a woman's connection to the deep feminine within herself has been damaged.

When rooted in the source of our female nature, the bodily and emotional suffering that we endure as women transforms into empathy toward others in their humanness. Compassion is a feature of the feminine. The word "passion" comes from Latin "pati" which means "to suffer." The prefix "com" also has Latin roots; it means "together" or "in association with." Compassion therefore means "to suffer with" or "to suffer alongside."

We are not to take on the hardships of a man in our life, but we can feel with him when he is bewildered about what we mean, what we want, or how he needs to respond to us. Often, he truly doesn't know what we mean or want, even though we've told him a thousand times. He *wants* to please us, but his brain doesn't work the same way ours does. We perceive things that he does not, and cannot, see. We understand in ways that he does not, and cannot, grasp. Our impatience with his differentness causes unnecessary suffering.

A man *wants* us to trust him, to believe in him. When we don't, he hurts. When we are displeased with him, he hurts. We can come alongside him in his suffering without rescuing or excusing him, just accompanying him. Tenderness and patience then bloom within us and the relationship may be healed.

With a display of this kind of femininity, we give a man, whether inside us or outside, something to respond to. His masculinity is called forth.

In the presence of that masculinity, we know ourselves more fully, experience our femininity more completely. Both he, the man, and we, the woman, encounter a moment where it is safe to be known. One where we catch a glimmer of who we really are, where we thrill to the Being of who we really are.

This is intimacy. It is an exchange between a rooted, receptive, ready feminine and a received, respected, responsive masculine. This dynamic is archetypal, meaning that it has been present from the beginning of humanity.

The biblical story of Adam and Eve portrays the natural interplay between the feminine and the masculine energies in the human psyche. The feminine awakens the masculine to the inner life of emotion and care while masculine responsiveness opens the eyes—the perception—of the feminine to who she is. Here is my paraphrase of the story:

Once upon a time in a garden named Eden, there walked a woman who had no shame, self-doubt, or fear. She shared this place of mist and fruit and birdsong with a man who knew no anger, no worry, no anxiety.

Every evening, a big burly Presence joined them for chitchat and laughter. Usually, this Presence seemed generous and loving; sometimes it was moody, and sometimes it issued rules and ultimatums. Yet still, there was no alienation or loneliness. Things were just fun, loving, warm, and close, with an occasional rumbling about rules—especially about a certain tree in the garden.

One day, in the middle of the day—in the middle of its usual playfulness—the woman ran to the tree, calling to Adam, "How many apples are on the tree today?"

A serpent of substance, its body curled around a branch of the tree, lowered its head so that it looked the woman in the eye. "Don't just count the apples," it said, "taste one."

"Oh, I can't do that!" said the woman. But before the words were out of her mouth, she realized that tasting might be what those apples were for.

She reached up, closed her hand around a firm shape, and tugged. The apple was in her hand. She took a bite. It was crisp. Sweet. Juicy.

"Adam!" she called. "There's one less apple on the tree. Come taste it!"

He looked at her. Looked at the red apple with a white scoop in it.

"Try it," the woman said. "It's REALLY good. Not like anything we've tasted."

Between the two of them, they ate it, core and all.

When evening came, things did not feel like they usually did. "Uh-oh," the couple whispered to each other. "We weren't supposed to . . ."

And the Presence thundered, "Have you done what we agreed you would NOT do?"

The woman thought, "I don't think we agreed. *"*

Adam said, "The woman you made tempted me."

The woman said, "The serpent deceived me." Yet inside herself, she knew that she had chosen to taste the apple.

The serpent raised its head and looked at the Presence eye-to-eye.

The Presence roared, "I punish you, Serpent! I punish you, Adam! I punish you, Woman! Out of my garden! Out of my sight! NOW!" The Presence withdrew, taking the mist with it.

An apple fell from the tree, making a little thud as it hit the ground. The birdsong around them ceased. Adam took the woman's hand, and she turned to face him. Their hearts were pounding.

Adam cleared his throat. "Woman, I name you Eve," he said. "I name you Eve, for you are the mother—the source—of all that lives."

In this tale, Eve takes a bite of the fruit plucked from the forbidden Tree of Knowledge. She offers it to Adam, who then takes a bite as well. Right away, both of them realize two things: that they are naked, and that they have disobeyed. Thus begins the stirring of consciousness in humanity.

Adam, the original masculine, woke up to the feminine, and then awakened the feminine to herself by naming what he saw. With awe in his voice, he said to this woman with whom he walked the Garden, "I name you Eve, for you are the mother of all."

This is a big moment.

When Adam perceived the deeper meaning of his human companion, the first name that he had given her—Woman—seemed unsuitable. It was the name of a kind of human, like a zebra or an elephant is a kind of animal. It was a name that identified her as part of him—as being made of man—rather than acknowledging who she was: the mother of all living things.

The story of Adam and Eve reveals truths about human life in a symbolic way. No individual woman is the mother of all living things, but the feminine nature within a woman does conceive, carry, birth, and nourish life in various ways.

Likewise, at the human level and in a much smaller and more personal manner, the masculine nature in a man is able to see something in a woman that she cannot see herself. Naming that something may open the woman's eyes to herself; it is a gift that a man can offer to a woman.

Such namings have occurred throughout my life. As I mentioned in Chapter Two, a psychiatrist once told me what he saw: that I was rejecting my own feminine self while having to navigate the world in a female body. It was eye-opening.

After a rigorous round of oral exams during my training to become a Jungian analyst, one of the examiners observed, "You don't let us see what you know." Although I had passed all the exams, his observation landed with such truth that it is seared into my consciousness. As I write this book, it peeps at me, reminding me to write what I know rather than mimicking someone else's take on things.

The man whose naming was the most important for me was my father. He received a terminal diagnosis during my year of solitary retreats. As Thanksgiving approached, my siblings and I gathered to be with our parents, and I received this impactful naming. As soon as I returned to Calgary, I went to my retreat cabin where I walked and cried and journaled this moment that was so precious to me.

Solitude – I Am Seen

Journal Entry

The last evening, I was alone in the house with Mom and Dad. It was the first chance we'd had to sit face-to-face, just the three of us. I sat in a low rocking chair in front of them; they rested in their recliners, both with their feet up. We talked about superficial things, personal things. We talked about heavier topics like death. We cried.

Then, words that surprised me came out of my mouth: I said to Dad that if he had anything to say to his children, if there was anything he wanted to pass on to his grandchildren, now was the time to do it.

He perked up. He looked me in the eye and said, "Peggy, you need to write. You have some books inside you, and you need to get them written. Do it now. I don't know a lot about writers, but from what I do know, they seem to need solitude to write. Get the solitude you need. Quit your job if you have to."

I was stunned. I never felt that Dad knew me or noticed me much, yet now he sat before me, issuing what I felt to be a blessing of the elder on his firstborn. My spirit quivered with pleasure. Surprise struck me dumb. His words reverberated within me: "You have books inside you that you must write..."

After saying our farewells, I floated out to my car,

then dashed back inside to give Mom and Dad one more goodnight/goodbye hug.

Again, I reached my car without my feet touching the ground. As I turned from their driveway onto the street, I rolled down my window, stuck my arm out, and waved.

I left my window open all the way to Sis's house, driving with my head out the window, baptized by the light of stars and the breeze of a night that loved me. I thought this trip was about saying goodbye to my father; in the end, he opened a door to the universe for me.

An emotional response is usually a woman's surest guide to what belongs to her. I heard my father's words as affirming something that belonged to me, and perhaps something to which I could belong. There was no lack of emotion within me.

When the animus, the inner man, is still uneducated, it may use what the outer man says as ammunition to undermine the woman. Any of the examples given above in which men's comments showed me something about myself could have been taken in a negative way—as criticism or admonition. We women must teach the animus to listen, to withhold judgment and wait while we bring our feminine perspective and understanding to what we just heard.

Through this process, the animus gets to know us, and we get to know ourselves better.

With a mutual knowledge of who we are, shared between our ego and the animus, protection from within becomes possible. For instance, the pairing of ego and animus helps us remain invisible when we have no resources for dealing with the outer world—when, like the moon, we are in withdrawal phase, seeing too much truth about our lives. The outer world may judge us for hiding away, but the inner world will not. Instead, we may experience the animus as putting a blanket around us, patting our shoulder, and saying, "Now, now. In time, you will know what to do." In fact, we might be persuaded to marry an inner guy like that, which is the whole point of establishing a relationship with the animus: to have an inner partner.

Much has been written about the negative animus, the one that gives us so much trouble. Little is written about the positive animus. I'm hungry to know what it is like.

My own animus has calmed down a lot. Sometimes, we dance together.

I once had a dream in which I sat in the front pew of a church. On the stage, a black man danced with a woman in an orange dress. He showed such tenderness toward her, and she was so softly receptive to him. As I observed them, I knew there would be a child, and that the child would be fully received by both.

The dream left me with a feeling of reverence. The church setting lent an air of holiness to it despite the colours of Halloween, which may have been a representation of the union of opposites: male and female, the sacred and the mundane, death and life, ghosts and goodies.

I painted a picture of that couple, with the woman relaxing into the man's sheltering body. She is looking down at her belly that's just starting to curve out with baby; he is gazing down at her with an equal glow of love. This crude painting is on the cover of this book. The images I draw or paint usually have a primitive feel to them and therefore can be rather off-putting, but they rise from deep inside me and express the essence of what came to me and moved me. This is what we need to do with the images, happenings, and insights that speak to us and even alter us in some way: we need to bring them into our reality and find a concrete way to keep them with us in our days.

Two other pictures of dancers hang on the wall in my writing room; the physical acts of the dancers reflect the psychological functions of the inner man.

In the first image, a black man sits on the floor, legs straight out in front of him, anchoring the feet of his female partner in his crotch; his arms encircle her knees as she bends backward, hair and fingers touching the floor. When viewed from the perspective of the inner world, we see that the animus secures a woman's stance—keeping her feet on the ground—as her mind swoops in an arc between A and B. A woman's mind does not travel in a linear fashion. It curves to and from the underworld, touching the upper world on its way. A woman's thinking thus feeds off itself, receiving hunches, insights, and foresight from the inner realm while also participating in the outer world of happenings and activities. This natural process of information flowing back and forth between worlds results in feminine understanding.

Even that description is an example of feminine thinking: a bit convoluted, circling as it tries to express the nature of a woman's mind. In my search for language that would capture feminine thinking, the animus-awareness within me kept pulling my focus back to what I was trying to convey: the psychological meaning of the female dancer's arched body. This consistent focal point of the animus was helpful.

In the picture, the male dancer embraces the woman's knees. Without those muscular, bracing arms, she cannot go into the backward arc that leaves her hands free. The animus gives a steadying, grounding support to a woman's flexible thinking that informs her handling of the world. The positive animus holds her standpoint stable. The woman can trust him, rely on him, rest in his belief in her. He shores her up rather than tearing her down. Instead of pushing her, he waits for her. This is representative of an outer man who clues into the femininity of his woman. The expressions of her ideas, her attempts at explaining something, are likely to be rather circular. He is patient, tries to listen beneath her words because what she is really saying may not be clear even to her. Or, she may know what she is trying to convey but doesn't have the language for it. English is short on words that express feminine knowings and sensibilities.

A responsive man names his take on what she's saying in a tentative way. Sometimes this clarifies things for her, sometimes it doesn't. It may simply leave her feeling heard, which is a lot. And often, it is enough.

The second picture on my wall shows a black man in a half-squat, long legs bent, knees spread. A woman rests on his thighs, her legs stretch outward into a split, toes pointed. The man's arms encircle her waist. Both look at the camera with complete poise.

This is a strong figure of the constructive animus that stands behind a woman's interests and values. He has her back, and she rests on the base he provides. She knows he will not suddenly stand up and dump her—their trusting collaboration enables her to be in the world with composure and self-assurance.

One thing that strikes me about the pose of this female dancer is its openness. Her legs are wide open. Her clothed chest is visible. Her eyes are direct and unveiled, without fear.

A woman who feels safe with her outer man will be relaxed in his presence—vulnerable and trusting. She is receptive, which means she has a good connection with her inner feminine. It also means that her outer man relates to her in a manner that makes her feel secure with him, both physically and emotionally.

His responses show consideration of her. For example, many women who watch sports with their husbands do so not because they're interested in sports, but rather because they want to be with him. The responsive man refrains from channel surfing during commercials and instead talks with his woman about whatever—perhaps the game or something that she brings up. While chatting, he looks at her, not at the TV or his phone or the commercials. Even better, he mutes the TV. Such responses acknowledge her presence and her importance to him.

A woman needs to be treated like she exists in her own right, not just for her man's convenience. Like she's on his radar. Like she's special to him. He, after all, chose her.

Simple courtesies count. He tucks a throw around her when she is chilly instead of tossing the throw to her. He cleans up after himself—his laundry, his dishes, his newspaper—and sometimes after her too. He keeps his promises. He comes home when he said he would, takes care of the things he said he would look after, checks with her before making commitments that will affect her.

These thoughtful deeds require effort on his part—ongoing effort.

When they are done without impatience or moodiness, they pay off. When they are done with respect and appreciation, they pay off. The woman begins to experience her worth to the man and a basis for trusting him is built—a foundation from which she can open her heart and her body to him.

A responsive masculine, whether inner or outer, accepts the ways of the feminine without judgment, even welcomes them in their differentness from his maleness. Therefore, the animus finds its proper place when it stops criticizing and belittling the woman from within. When its attitude is one of devotion to the woman whose psyche it inhabits, the two can then dance—animus and woman. The inner masculine steadies the female ego in its flexibility. It showcases her litheness in dealing with what her days bring, her nimbleness in relating, her agility in thinking and comprehending and speaking. As a partner, the animus holds the woman in the same way a male ballet dancer lifts, carries, and catches his ballerina.

Similar to the male dancers in the photographs I described, the animus follows the timing of its female partner. Like them, it offers support in moves and positions that put the feminine forward.

The men in the pictures are black; this detail applies to the animus in that it lives and functions in the unconscious of a woman. The role of the male dancers is also that of the inner masculine: both belong behind and under the woman's ego, in service to her feminine nature and what she needs in the moment.

Solitude – Gallantry

I walk up to the gazebo. Standing by myself on the hill, feeling the wind in my hair and the sun on my face, hearing the frogs in the distance, I feel very alone—a feeling that seems to be a frequent visitor these days.

The loneliness has a nebulous quality to it; I can't pinpoint its cause. Being in the presence of other people doesn't alleviate it. In fact, chitchatting with others seems to stir it up.

The wind on the hilltop tugs at my jacket, my jeans. Keeps my hair in motion. Tucks my loneliness inside me, like being at a fresh gravesite where everyone has downcast eyes, hearts that can't beat without aching. Everyone alone in their loneliness.

I close my eyes and lift my face to the wind, remembering the funerals I've attended. There was always wind at the graveside.

I think of my parents, knowing that their days on earth are numbered. I can't imagine them being gone, can't fathom what it will be like to be on this earth without them.

And then I remember a trip home a few years ago. Mom and Dad had been married for sixty years at the time and were going through a thorny patch due to my mother's declining health. On that visit, Mom's body seemed shriveled with pain. Her mind was forgetting things that Dad always depended on her to remember. Her energy gave out by mid-morning. She sometimes snapped at Dad, expecting more of him than he could deliver and then criticizing him for it.

I noticed him hustling to Mom's every beck and call, submitting himself to her impossible demands. By a few days into the visit, this was getting to me. I wondered why he didn't stand up for himself. Why was he so passive?

Finally, I followed him into the screened porch at the back of the house and watched him open the freezer to find something Mom wanted. I asked, "What are you doing, Dad?" He knew what I meant.

Turning from the freezer, he looked at me with moist eyes.

"Daughter," he said in a gentle voice, "your mother hurts so bad she can't think straight. Me refusing to do as she asks would just add to her suffering. She isn't herself, and I don't want you, or anyone, to see her like this."

My heart squeezed with tenderness and tears. *He really, really loves her*, I thought.

He leaned back against the freezer and held my gaze for a few seconds. His eyes looked so sad. "What you see here on this visit is not the woman I have been married to all these years. That woman loved me. She loved me fiercely and faithfully and fully.

"I still love that woman, and *she's* the one I am serving."

He went back to looking for whatever he came to find in the freezer.

What at first looked like passive behaviour turned out to be conscious devotion. My elderly father knew what he was doing and for whom he was doing it. He had my mother's back in a very private way, protecting her reputation with others. Protecting her dignity.

This was a show of compassion in a masculine manner. He had a loving heart that could not be corrupted by the vagaries of life. He saw through the veil of his wife's agony to her natural beauty and goodness. Though my mother was beside herself with suffering, my father still supported her from below on a platform made of masculine strength—like the male dancer holding himself still in a half-squat beneath the female performer, whose role required his steady position.

A responsive (as opposed to a reactive) masculine is one who has listened to his woman. One who has taken what she said over the years seriously, has paid attention to the things that matter to her even though they seem small and insignificant to him. One who has noticed the truth, the "rightness," of her way of seeing and knowing that is so different from his way of understanding things. Such a man, whether inner or outer, knows the woman and can give himself to her without diminishing himself. There is no recipe for this masculine care, for it comes out of his individuality in response to her individuality.

Years ago, a man identified a responsiveness in my husband that I had not recognized. While Steve was a seminary student, he and I participated in a therapy group for couples offered through the school. In that group, I spoke of my struggles with the dictates given to wives by the Bible and the church. I openly questioned whether the silence and submissiveness expected of women were biblical or if they were cultural. Did those guidelines really come from God, or were they society's ideas parading as God's commands?

This was quite unsettling for the group. During a break one evening, a male group member and I were alone for a moment. He said, "I very much admire your courage in questioning what we've all been taught, and you need to know how special your husband is."

I looked at him quizzically. I didn't get the connection between my courage and my husband being special. It did indeed take courage to do what I was doing; my questioning felt dangerous to me, and none of the other women in the group were speaking up. But what made Steve "special?"

The man leaned close and quietly said, "I would never ever allow my wife to ask such a question. Never. It takes a special man to tolerate that in a wife."

With those words, I realized that Steve too was being brave. I, his wife, was breaking with centuries of teachings by the very religion that had drawn us to each other, had shaped our marriage, and in which he now hoped to become a minister. Yet not once had he told me to stop exploring or caution me to stay quiet. He was not only "special" but also wise. If Steve had not made space for my intellectual and psychological explorations, he would have lost me to either depression or divorce.

An inner masculine whose allegiance lies with the individual woman rather than the collective views of society or religion behaves much like my father did in protecting my mother's reputation, or like my husband did in respecting my necessary explorations. Transformed from tormentor to the woman's best ally, the animus stands behind her ego, invisibly backing her up in all that she does, feels, and says.

Proper male responsiveness starts with our own attitude toward the feminine within ourselves. We must respect our personal rhythms, value our feminine intelligence, and trust our inner timing. We must understand what belongs to us and what doesn't. We must identify what's important to us and what's not. It is in getting to know and appreciate our feminine core that we extend a hand to the inner man and begin to bring him into partnership. Through this union, we move from opinions and fears about the world to experiencing life as sacred, even when it is routine and tedious. This produces a spiritual firmness that brings meaning and purpose to every part of our day. We are then prepared to receive and guide our outer man.

In the natural world, the cow does not despise the virility of the bull, nor does she envy it. Her inner readiness draws the bull to her as his opposite while her instinctual timing opens her to the potency of his fertilizing activity. Likewise, we do not need to be militant or clashing or castrating, nor do we need to explain, apologize, or grovel. Being rooted in the deep feminine makes it possible for us to use playfulness and feeling without being defensive. Asserting ourselves in this manner invites connection while preserving our true nature.

A psychological law exists between the archetypal masculine and feminine. The receptive nature of the feminine attracts, arouses, and engages the masculine. The penetrating nature of the masculine focuses, initiates, and acts. With their objective and rational outlook, men can bring to our awareness things that our feminine nature does not perceive; their observations and questions sharpen our thinking, clarify what we're trying to say. We broaden their understanding when we put forward what we see, think, feel, and know. Accepting and expressing our feminine nature sustains us in the face of patriarchal attitudes.

Reclaiming what has been wrongfully taken from a woman's sense of herself as feminine involves suffering, wandering, and endurance. Authentic womanhood springs from a rootedness in her body, her instincts, and her emotions. Plumbing these depths as adults brings forth a wise timing and a compassionate heart that fulfills the essence of the natural feminine: relatedness. From this state of readiness, a well-developed feminine can engage a robust masculine. With every woman who achieves this inner partnership—or even works toward such alliance—*equality of value* in the world of men becomes more possible.

Afterword

This book opened with cows and bulls being placed in the barnyard on the playmat attached to the wall above my laptop. Those pastures are now empty. All the cows and bulls have exited the farm and travelled down the lane to my publisher, and from there to you.

What I have learned from the cow and the bull is that their natures need each other. One cannot be whole without the other. Without the bull, the circling and cycling of the cow comes to naught; feminine fertility lies fallow. Without the cow, the bull's virility and vitality wastes itself, tossed to the wind like confetti.

In simple terms, without the masculine, things don't get done; without the feminine, things are not experienced. And to be a whole person living life fully, we need to experience what we do.

As the carriers of the feminine, we women must not leave the masculine alone, without feedback, without input. We must not view the masculine as the enemy but rather as an ally. Befriending the inner masculine enables a woman to meet the outer masculine—be that an individual man or a patriarchal society—as an equal, giving him a feminine presence to whom he can respond. From such a partnership, a new world can be born where men feel valued in their masculinity and women are valued in our femininity. A world where both are able to walk this earth unharmed, where life on Earth thrives.

The feminine pole in the psyche animates or enlivens all of life. It contains an ancient intelligence that instructs us through the body and awakens a longing for union with our own divinity. This feminine knowing does not come from the mind, nor from above, nor from what we typically call enlightenment. It comes from below, from a potent source that dwells in the darkness of the earth, in the human body, and in the unconscious. A dream I once had offers an image of how the feminine deep within us works:

A stream flows inside a deep cave that is very dim and quiet. A bamboo bridge spans the stream, one end of it near me, the other barely visible as it extends into the dark reaches of the cavern. To my right and some distance away, two men are fishing with rods and bait—one old, the other young.

Out of the deep darkness at the back of the cave, a young woman emerges and steps onto the bridge. As she comes toward me, I see that she is dressed in a pale dusky-rose sundress. Her hair is loose and dark and falls about her shoulders. She is barefoot. As she steps off the bridge, she turns to my left.

The men have seen her and keep glancing at her as they cast their lines, reel them in, and cast again. They have not caught any fish.

Suddenly, on the woman's side of the bridge, a fish leaps out of the water, gleaming silver in the dimness, and then it is gone. The woman bends down, plunges both hands into the water, and brings up the fish.

I keep on my desk a small silver frame that holds a tiny sketch of a fish leaping out of the water. It reminds me of the dream in which I witnessed the way of the feminine, which is natural and hidden. The masculine fishes for sustenance through tools of its own making; the feminine, being conversant with the depths, does not need such manmade means. She can go where the masculine cannot go. Able to see in the dark, able to breathe underwater, able to find what lies on the seabed of the unconscious, the feminine collects treasures and knowledge from the recesses of the psyche, then returns to the surface and offers these nourishing nuggets to humanity.

This is the power of the feminine. She knows from below, and she brings a "knowing" to us as women. Furthermore, she "gets" us, comprehends us, both individually and collectively. The knowledge that comes from her is tailor-made to the moment and to the person, and trusting this knowing delivers us into our feminine power. This is not a power over, nor is it a power for or against. It is a power to stand in and live out of, in service to life.

My dear sisters, the feminine lives in our bodies. We are her warm human hands, her bright laughter, her inclusive voice, her intelligent heart. Let's return to our roots and become fully Woman.

Appendix A

The Seneca Healing Quest

Throughout time, Indigenous peoples all over the world have performed rites of passage to help girls experience themselves as women at the time of menarche—the time when their periods begin. A First Nations band in North America, the Seneca tribe, engages in one such practice which serves to return the woman to harmony with her natural feminine state. This ritual, called the Healing Quest, can be undertaken at any time in a woman's life and as often as needed.

The Seneca people are part of the Iroquois Confederacy of Six Nations primarily situated around the Great Lakes. Other bands include the Onondaga, Mohawk, Oneida, Cayuga, and Tuscarora. These clans share a common government and matrilineal system in which women are viewed as the stewards of the land. A woman is the holder of her family's dwelling, horses, and farmland. The work of her hands is hers to do with as she chooses. Social status originates in the female side of the lineage. A woman can ask her husband to leave, and the children stay with her.

While the public leaders of these people are men, they are elected and advised by the women. Ignoring the guidance of the Clan Mothers—becoming corrupt or refusing to listen to the people—is grounds for stripping the man of his position.

In these tribes, there is equitable valuing of both women and men. The differences between the sexes are acknowledged without being judged as lacking or desirable; the differences simply exist and are worked with rather than against. This dynamic of accepting and complying with natural differences shows itself in the cultural rites surrounding manhood and womanhood.

Boys undergo the Warrior Way of initiation through a Vision Quest. Being demonstrative by nature, a male must stop all activity, face fear, and experience the deprivation of food, water, and sleep in order to open the male ego to the feminine side. To go beyond any limitation, the active masculine principle must be forced to be st

This rite involves being accompanied into Nature by an elder, wh then leaves the boy alone after instructing him on what to expect. A state of receptivity is reached through being alone in the wilderness and yearning for a vision to guide him through the trial. Receiving a vision not only completes the quest but also provides the boy with spiritual companionship and a sense of purpose. It empowers him by strengthening his ego's connection to the spirit world, providing a grounding from which the youth can move into the responsibilities of manhood.

The Seneca understanding is that the male ego has to be broken down through fear and deprivation in order for the boy to receive a vision personal to him. A female, on the other hand, is believed to be visionary by nature. Women hold their visions inside themselves, in their womb space. What women need is respite from the constant dependency of others on them.

In ancient times, Seneca women did not go on Vision Quests. Instead, their people offered Healing Quests, which were taken any time a woman needed. The understanding was that women suffer enough during their menstrual cycles, pregnancy, labour, and birth. In nurturing the young, caring for the ill, and accompanying the old through death, women undergo hardship and deprivation. They face death, they face fear, and they often go without sleep, food, and water as they tend to the critical needs of others.

Because women are naturally visionary and spiritually sensitive, they are seen as the keepers of culture and the carriers of soul. They bring a creative force to the collective—to their families, to their communities, and to humanity itself. Their presence enlivens the environment around them, be it the home, the communal firepit, the workplace, the church, the market, or the bedroom. Women therefore need protection and support rather than the physical and psychological challenges of a Vision Quest.

In the Seneca tradition, the Healing Quest involves taking a minimum of three full days of solitude every four weeks, without fail,

; this happens during the menstrual period; if the ...r bleeds due to menopause or a hysterectomy, she ...ntime cycle (often the full or new moon).

, this monthly retreat from the responsibilities of her daily ..., a woman withdraws into herself, replenishing her body with rest, opening her heart to Nature's rhythms, allowing her mind to play. It is a time for the woman to be filled, fed, rejuvenated, and nurtured. Light food and clean water need to be available so that the woman can eat whenever she is hungry and drink whenever she is thirsty. The clock is to be turned to the wall, and all reading material, music with words, television, and internet are made unavailable. A warm, comfortable shelter frees her to relax and slow down. She needs to roam in a safe place, free of artificial distractions such as traffic, social media, and the news. This is a time for the woman to de-stress and become attuned to herself.

The only activities to take place while on retreat are ones of the woman's own making: singing, drumming, dancing, giving thanks, creating poetry, drawing, writing, walking, pondering, gathering rocks, sitting, and daydreaming. The point is to fill herself up with self-expression and thanks-giving. Anything that stresses her body, mind, or heart wastes her time and energy and keeps her from receiving what wants to rise up from within her.

After a year of this special time, a woman has learned to trust herself. She becomes comfortable being alone, discovers her body's natural rhythms, and opens to the receptive side of herself.

The entire process of taking these monthly solitudes is a major commitment to herself that enables the woman to receive from Nature the same quality of healing and nurturing that she gives to others. It teaches her to honour and love herself, to recognize the beauty within herself, and to reclaim the magic and mystery of the feminine.

The Healing Quest comes to a close with the thirteenth solitude. A female elder watches over the woman during those three days and nights. Every day, the women of her clan prepare food and place it just outside her shelter. At the end of that solitude, they pack and carry her belongings back to the common house. Under the guidance of the elder, the Quester shares with her women-companions the vision(s) that she has received. Together, they discern the meaning and usefulness of the vision(s) for the rest of the tribe.

Seneca women still undertake Healing Quests to this day.

Appendix B

My Thoughts on Transgender

I know what it is like to live in a body that I do not value, but I do not know what it's like to live in a body that feels wrong. It is not fair for me to pretend to have answers for people who know they are in the wrong body. However, for those who are confused about whether they should identify as male or female, who do not know whether they are in the right body, I do have a suggestion. Work at getting to know the masculine or feminine part of your psyche—whichever is opposite the sex of your body. Perhaps that will bring some clarity to your predicament.

Whether transgender or cisgender, each of us needs to get to know the part of ourselves that is opposite to the sex of our body. A woman can more readily take a stand in the outer world when she has a relationship with her inner masculine. That inner support generates confidence in her way of Doing and Being. A man who is in touch with his inner woman expresses the tenderness and emotional responsiveness of the feminine in a masculine way. Manly femininity is beautiful to behold and electrifying to experience.

Perhaps developing a relationship with the opposite-sex energies within one's psyche can help an individual settle into an identity. Achieving this is much like establishing a friendship with another person; it takes time, curiosity, respect, honesty, and a consistent and repeated dialogue. In a friendship—whether inner or outer—we come to know the other as well as ourselves.

Friendship provides support, stability, protection, and love; befriending our inner masculine or inner feminine does the same thing from within. This strengthens us and assures us, and so the outer world becomes a more livable place.

When we feel intact on the inside, identifying ourselves by sex matters less. We are who we are and can live who we are without taking offense at or feeling shaken by gendered pronouns. Embodying the psychological characteristics of both the masculine and the feminine brings us closer to wholeness in our human experiences and responses, no matter the body sex.

Acknowledgements

Ten years ago, my friend Susan Cullen heard my lecture on this topic. She told me then, and continued to remind me over monthly breakfasts, that it was worthy of a book. I am grateful that she did not give up.

Susan also clued me onto Influence Publishing, where I found Julie Ann —the editor who saw, more clearly than I could, the potential and value in what I proposed. Enthusiastic and wise, Julie Ann guided me away from a "scientific" voice toward a more personal and feminine voice. As a result, this feels like *my* book as opposed to *a* book. Her enthusiasm kept me going.

My content editor, Danielle Anderson polished the manuscript into a smoother read. Her astute comments and questions both clarified and tightened what I attempted to say in this book. Thanks also to my proofreader, John De Freitas, for his thorough work. As well, it has been a pleasure to work with the expert and dedicated team at Influence Publishing.

A heartfelt shout-out to my farmer-rancher friend Roger Hiebert who gave me straightforward information about cows and bulls. The wisdom and humility of lived experience filled his word-pictures with humour, affection, and keen observations. In talking with Roger, animal nature came to life for me.

Special gratitude goes to my dear Karen Kurtz. Your observations about the value of my solitary experiences, not only for myself but for other women as well, gave me purpose in writing this book.

Thank you to my readers Kim Blight, Rose Raimondo, Matthew Brace, Annette Bossert, and Susan Cullen. Your perspectives revealed blind spots and assumptions as well as what worked and why. My monthly writers' group encouraged me through sharing their own struggles, blocks, advances, and ways of including fun. Warm thanks to Selena Bloom, Matthew Brace, Dale Forsberg, and Niobe Weaver.

To the women of my spirituality group who met during my year of solitudes: Suzanne Rosebrugh, Jean Mitchell, Marta Dixon, Janet Arnold, and Cheryl Lee Anderson – may you always have clitzpah!

My appreciation to Wendy Klassen, Natalie Owen, Sylvia Bates, Jane Smith-Eivemark, Pat Moran, and my sister Maxine Kirkpatrick for your friendship and unwavering interest; your company gave relief from the intensity of writing. I treasure the candid conversations about the confusions, yearnings, prohibitions and pleasures of our female lives that I've had with each and all of you.

My daughters-in-law, natives of China and Brazil, broadened and grounded my understanding of the feminine through the ways in which their cultural upbringings have been different from mine. In their natural styles of relating and dealing with life, they have shown an acceptance of instinct and feminine intelligence that I never imagined.

Support has come from my sons, who have modeled initiative in their creative pursuits and affirmed me in mine. The extent of their involvement in their marriages and in fathering their children gives me optimism for our future world. My husband continues to provide opportunities and room to grow into my feminine self, which I do not take for granted. He has been patient with the scarcity of my companionship as I wrote this book. Thank you, my men!

I see the prejudice and inequities that these men of mine sometimes encounter. My work toward women valuing the feminine is as much for them as it is for women. The burden of achieving an equity of value is shared by both men and women, and progress must be in service to equality for both.

Lastly, I acknowledge the feminine within me, although she sometimes drove me around the bend in her insistence that I stick close to her sense of things. She wanted realness and sincerity and truth, and so did I. Writing this book with her has been a rich journey.

Author Biography

Peggy Funk Voth is a clinical social worker and Jungian analyst in private practice. Her keen interest in the wholesome embodiment and expression of the masculine and feminine principles in everyday life informs her lectures, therapeutic work and gatherings of women. Peggy underwent thirteen solitudes in accordance with the Seneca Healing Quest that she describes in this book. She grew up on a farm in Texas, married a Canadian, became a mother, a grandmother and a dual citizen, and now lives with her husband in Calgary, Alberta.

Website: www.peggyvoth.com/
Facebook: www.facebook.com/peggyfunkvoth
LinkedIn: www.linkedin.com/in/peggy-voth-79721327